This exhibition and catalog have been made possible by a grant from the National Endowment for the Arts, a Federal agency, and support from the Museum's Modern and Contemporary Art Council.

California:
5 Footnotes to Modern
Art History

Morgan Russell: Unknown Paintings
Dynaton Revisited
Los Angeles Hard-Edge: The Fifties and the Seventies
John McLaughlin Letters and Documents
Environmental Communications Looks at Los Angeles

Foreword by Maurice Tuchman
Edited by Stephanie Barron

18 January-24 April 1977

Contemporary Art Galleries, Lytton Halls
Frances and Armand Hammer Wing
Los Angeles County Museum of Art

Los Angeles County Museum of Art

ISBN 0-87587-078-3

Library of Congress
Catalog Card Number 77-70284

Published by the
Los Angeles County Museum of Art
5905 Wilshire Boulevard
Los Angeles, California 90036

Copyright © 1977 by
Museum Associates of the
Los Angeles County Museum of Art

All rights reserved

Printed in the U.S.A.

Table of Contents

Illustrations

Foreword

Our anticipation of the College Art Association meeting in Los Angeles in February 1977 prompted us to apply to the National Endowment for the Arts for a grant that would allow us to provide our public, to be increased at that time by over 3,000 art historians, artists, and museum professionals, with stimulating material. It seemed appropriate to focus on California resources. The choice between a jubilee/roundup of Western styles and a modest focus upon several different, neglected aspects of California art history fell to the latter option, as it was deemed to be more pertinent. We imagine that much serious research at the graduate and post-doctoral level will be generated by a number of exhibitions which uncover the unknown (literally, in the case of the buried Morgan Russell paintings) and emphasize the less known.

We knew of the existence of Morgan Russsell's paintings in the estate of Los Angeles painter Stanton Macdonald-Wright, having seen them at the home of the latter's wife, Jean Macdonald-Wright. Included were Russell's Fauve-inspired paintings from around 1907; major Synchromist works of circa 1912; and the completely unknown figurative paintings, often of transvestites, painted in a style influenced by Greco-Roman frescoes. In addition, Mrs. Macdonald-Wright shared with us the fascinating correspondence between her husband, who was living in Santa Monica in the teens and twenties, and Russell, who was living outside of Paris. This material has been made available for this publication, and selections have been used by Gail Levin in her essay; the complete correspondence, along with Macdonald-Wright's diaries, will appear in a publication being edited by Mrs. Macdonald-Wright.

Dynaton was known to us as an interesting Bay Area alternative to the New York School of around 1950; we were not well versed in the achievement of the participating artists Lee Mullican, Gordon Onslow Ford, and Wolfgang Paalen until Los Angeles collectors Joann and Gifford Phillips showed us Sylvia Fink's Ph.D. dissertation from the University of Arizona. Visits to Onslow Ford and Mullican (Paalen died in 1959) immediately convinced us that their contribution to American post-War art should be reviewed.

Hard-edge painting has long been an identifying trait of Los Angeles art. This descriptive phrase first appeared in print in critic Jules Langsner's introduction to the catalog of LACMA's important 1959 exhibition titled *Four Abstract Classicists*. The exhibition then traveled to London's Institute of Contemporary Art, where Lawrence Alloway, then director, renamed the show *West Coast Hard-Edge*, thereby gaining international currency, perhaps for the first time, for a characteristic California art style. The hallmark of paintings by the four artists Karl Benjamin, Lorser Feitelson, Frederick Hammersley, and John McLaughlin is a blend of detached lyricism, consummate and immaculate execution, all infused by unworried confidence. This spirit came to characterize the justly celebrated Los Angeles look in the sixties, when a younger generation of first-rate talents including Robert Irwin, Larry Bell, Kenneth Price, Craig Kauffman, and Billy Al Bengston brought worldwide attention to Los Angeles as a major art center. We re-create here the *Four Abstract Classicists* exhibition and update it with work by the same artists from the seventies. The four essays attempt to assess the artists' careers in both decades.

John McLaughlin died in 1976, and in presenting a modest exhibition of his letters, photographs, and models, we wish to call attention to the profound respect McLaughlin enjoyed in his time and now in the Los Angeles art community. A figure, in our opinion, of world importance, we dedicated an exhibition in 1976 to his memory. Of the four Los Angeles painters in the exhibition *New Abstract Painting in Los Angeles,* on view in LACMA in late 1976, each asked us to have McLaughlin paintings from the permanent collection at the entrance to the show. Such is the feeling for John McLaughlin's achievement and for his example as an artist. All the material in this homage to him comes from the Archives of American Art, a branch of the Smithsonian Institution. With it we hope thereby to point out to California collectors and artists the importance of retaining the various evidences of their art experiences, and to scholars the availability of such material for research and study.

With the entrance of the group called Environmental Communications into Los Angeles in the late sixties, the self-conscious sense of history being made and recorded here became accentuated. With a passion verging on obsession this talented group has documented the visuals of Los Angeles lifestyles in a manner almost archeological in intent.

When the Department of Modern Art was founded at LACMA in 1964, our policy was to abandon regional presentations such as the Los Angeles County Annual, an open, juried show that had served to alienate any number of first-rate artists and mistakenly encourage scores of others. The new policy at the Museum was to exhibit contemporary art regardless of origin; the fact that the high percentage of art shown was from Los Angeles proved its quality, rather than reflected provincial favoritism on the part of the Museum. In the decade since that policy went into effect, Los Angeles art has so clearly made its mark that we now can confidently present these "footnotes" to modern art history with little fear that viewers will perceive California as less than the mainstream cultural environment it is.

Maurice Tuchman
Senior Curator, Modern Art
November 1976

Acknowledgments

Museum Director Kenneth Donahue welcomed our proposal for these special exhibitions for the CAA and was instrumental in helping us obtain the necessary NEA grant. We are grateful to the NEA for its sponsorship of the shows and the catalog. The Museum's Modern and Contemporary Art Council, the support arm of the Department of Modern Art, was helpful in many ways.

I directed each of these projects with the close association of Associate Curator of Modern Art Stephanie Barron. National Museum Art Intern Marie Cieri provided creative labor far beyond that which could be expected of an intern; her contribution was professional. Barbara McQuaide, long-time department secretary, managed as always to type sheaves of manuscripts while handling the incessantly ringing telephone lines. Departmental anchorwoman, Betty Asher, curatorial assistant, helped us all keep our wits about us, particularly with an eye to myriad customary duties. Cecil Fergerson, curatorial assistant in modern art, played a special role in relating to all the artists and their representatives in the staging of the exhibitions and the necessary rearrangement of the permanent collections. Kathy Zimmerer, special assistant, was helpful to the entire department during the preparatory stage of these exhibitions.

Finally, I must record the real pleasure I had in working with each of the artists, agents, art dealers, collectors, and the commissioned scholars and writers; Lee Mullican and Gordon Onslow Ford; Karl Benjamin, Lorser Feitelson, and Frederick Hammersley; Mrs. Stanton Macdonald-Wright; Randy Sprout; Nicholas Wilder; Robert Anthoine; Dr. Kenneth B. Bonilla; Mrs. Dolly Bright Carter; André Emmerich Gallery; David Greenberg, Elizabeth Freeman, and the staff of Environmental Communications; Paul Karlstrom and the Archives of American Art; Moses Lasky; Isabel Paalen; San Francisco Museum of Modern Art; Marian Willard; Van Deren Coke; Sylvia Fink; Susan C. Larsen; Gail Levin; Don McCallum; Diane Moran; Merle Schipper; and Tom Wolfe. Sue Foley and Jed Wilcox were especially helpful in providing photographs for the catalog.

M. T.

1.

Morgan Russell: Unknown Paintings

The paintings by Morgan Russell on view in this exhibition are being presented here for the first time in the United States. They were buried for decades in a tin crate in Hollywood, under the porch of a private home (see illustration). Stanton Macdonald-Wright has written the most complete account to date of this curious matter:

> The story of the buried crate of Russell's work is as follows: Russell sent to Frank L. Stevens [a journalist] a crate of pictures to be kept for him until he should send for them when he returned to France. Stevens buried the crate. In the crate, rolled up, was the original canvas 10½' x 7¼' [*sic*] of the "Synchromy in Blue-Violet," [in the current exhibition, cat. no. 2] shown by Russell in the Salon des Indépendents in 1913, a number of small pictures—figure work—and one small synchromy with, I believe, eight or ten very large figure works, some of whose reproductions I have, which were exhibited in Paris (ca.) 1930, and one large nude I saw him at work on in 1911-1912 in Paris, unfinished. This nude was painted on the back of a portrait of his wife, ca. 5' x 3' [cat. no. 1]. The portrait was in the Forum show in N.Y. in 1916 along with a number of other works. I was not present when the box was disinterred, about a year or so after the death of Mr. Stevens. The person who was there, one Harper, could tell more exactly the contents. He says his landlord gave away some works and he himself has at least one and I believe more.... I obtained possession of what pictures remained, which was seventeen. The story of how Russell tried several times, by mail, to obtain these pictures from Mr. Stevens, who finally denied he had them, is very strange. But I have letters from Russell asking for them. I believe the presently restored "Synchromy to Light," [*Synchromy in Blue-Violet*] 1912-13, to be Russell's greatest big canvas. There is one done a year later in Buffalo, even larger, same height but wider, that is inferior to the one here.

Mrs. Stanton Macdonald-Wright has given us permission to print this explanation; she has loaned us all the paintings in the exhibition (supplemented by one important Russell figurative painting of 1933 from LACMA's permanent collection, a gift from her late husband); and she has been unfailingly gracious and painstakingly scrupulous with her assistance and support throughout the preparation of the exhibition and catalog. Her representative Randy Sprout has also been of real assistance.

Gail Levin rapidly researched the voluminous materials we gave her to provide us with the most illuminating account and chronology of Russell's career to date. Ms. Levin is associate curator, Hopper Collection, Whitney Museum of American Art. She organized the exhibition *Morgan Russell: Synchromist Studies 1910-1922* at the Museum of Modern Art in Spring 1976, and is directing the forthcoming major exhibition *Synchromism and Color Abstraction, 1910-1925* scheduled for February 1978 at the Whitney Museum of American Art.

M. T.

The former Frank L. Stevens home,
Los Angeles, where Morgan Russell's
paintings were buried.

Morgan Russell: The Avant-Garde Dilemma

Gail Levin

Critics hailed him as an innovater [sic]. Then suddenly he changed style. He would not stay in one rut. The critics could not understand this, his desire for expansion and new life. He changed again and again because life was more important to him than esthetics.[1]

When these words describing Morgan Russell were published in the *Paris Times* of 31 January 1928, Russell was living with his wife on a farm in the small village of Aigremont, France. His pioneering work as a founder of Synchromism had been eclipsed if not completely forgotten. Russell barely managed to support himself and his wife through the sale of small paintings sent to California and sold there by his former colleague Stanton Macdonald-Wright.[2] In spite of the noisy attention his Synchromist work had received in 1913 and 1914, Russell, in 1928, remained aloof from the Paris art world.

Russell, who had first traveled to Paris from his native New York in 1906 at the age of twenty, settled there in 1909. During his first years in Paris, he had met Leo and Gertrude Stein, Matisse, Picasso, and Rodin. In New York he had first studied architecture. He then studied painting with Robert Henri and sculpture with James Earle Fraser. Russell pursued his study of sculpture in Paris with Matisse and concentrated on this medium until the fall of 1910. He then studied color theory with the Canadian artist Ernest Percyval Tudor-Hart (1873-1954). By 1911, he had met Stanton Macdonald-Wright, another aspiring young American artist. Russell was intensely aware of the most avant-garde events in Paris. He saw the Futurists' exhibition at the Bernheim-Jeune Gallery in February of 1912. The Futurists' outspoken manifestos and their bold Paris exhibition became a model for Russell's own plan to create an original art form.[3]

As early as July 1912, Russell was working toward the realization of "a new school" or "a new vision in painting." In his notebook of this period he composed a letter to his patron Mrs. Gertrude Vanderbilt Whitney in which he explained that he planned to distinguish himself from all the other Americans in Paris who were only "trying to equal in a small way some older work."[4] In his notebook of August 1912, he reminded himself to tell Mrs. Whitney that he hoped for an exhibition in Paris and that his "ambition will not stop at anything else." Thus, with the Synchromist exhibition at the Bernheim-Jeune Gallery in October 1913, a little more than a year later, Russell's expressed hopes were realized.

Stanton Macdonald-Wright joined Russell and they exhibited together as Synchromists. Their first exhibition occurred in June of 1913 in Munich at Der Neue Kunstsalon. Years later Macdonald-Wright recalled: "We only went there in the way that theatrical companies go out of town for a tryout."[5]

Similar to Russell's early Synchromies exhibited in Munich is his *Untitled (Synchromist Nude)* (cat. no. 1) ca. 1913. This painting contains both a recognizable figure and a still life arrangement. The figure is constructed of juxtaposed areas of bright, prismatic colors which animate the entire composition. Russell had begun to segment the background of the right side into brightly colored wedge shapes similar to those that appear in his more abstract Synchromies of 1913 and 1914. The unresolved nature of this painting is indicated by Russell's use of the verso of the canvas to paint a somber portrait of Emilie Francesconi (his future wife) in 1915. Exhibited in New York in the Forum Exhibition in 1916 as *Portrait of a Lady,* this gray painting is striking

---

1.
Paris Times, 31 January 1928, anonymous article on Russell.
2.
This help is detailed in the two artists' unpublished letters during the 1920s. I wish to thank both Mrs. Stanton Macdonald-Wright for making these letters and other information available to me and Mme. Morgan Russell for allowing me to quote from Russell's writings.
3.
The various Futurist manifestos and catalogs owned by Morgan Russell are now in the Lydia and Harry L. Winston Collection (Dr. and Mrs. Barnett Malbin, New York).

4.
Morgan Russell, unpublished notebook, dated July 1912. These and other Morgan Russell notebooks are in the collection of Mrs. and Mrs. Henry M. Reed, Caldwell, N.J. A number of the notebooks were included in the exhibition *Morgan Russell: Synchromist Studies 1910-1922,* Museum of Modern Art, New York, 1976, organized by the author. For further information, see the author's article "Morgan Russell's Notebooks: An American Avant-garde Painter in Paris," *RACAR,* Fall 1976, Bicentennial Issue.
5.
"Stanton Macdonald-Wright Interviewed by Frederick Wight" in *Stanton Macdonald-Wright —A Retrospective Exhibition 1911-1970,* The UCLA Art Galleries, Los Angeles, 1970.

in its lack of color. As Russell had written to Mrs. Whitney in 1915, he had found it necessary to give up his "vivid color work" of the previous winter due to eye strain and headaches.[6]

Included in the Bernheim-Jeune exhibition was one very large, purely abstract painting *Synchromie en bleu violacé (Synchromy in Blue-Violet)* (cat. no. 2) measuring 10'4'' by 7'6'', along with *Esquisse pour la Synchromie en bleu violacé (Sketch for Synchromy in Blue-Violet)* which was a study for the large painting. A handwritten list (in English and in French) that Russell made of the paintings in the Munich exhibition of the previous June indicates that several works shown, such as *Skizze in Violetteblau (Sketch in Blue-Violet)*, may have been related to *Synchromie en bleu violacé.*[7] Willard Huntington Wright, Stanton Macdonald-Wright's brother and a spokesman for the two Synchromists, wrote that "there were canvases in the Munich exhibition which were almost unrecognizable as nature," but that the first "wholly abstract canvas" was not exhibited until the Bernheim-Jeune exhibition."[8]

Writing about his abstract Synchromies to Stanton Macdonald-Wright on 20 October 1925, Russell revealed the importance that he had come to place on his *Synchromie en bleu violacé:*

> I've learned and realized lately that that picture was the beginning and end of that art as far as I'm concerned and that I should have gone on doing others, not on the same motif, but on the idea, the same general proportional feeling...

Although the *Synchromie en bleu violacé* was previously thought to have been destroyed, it was rediscovered (literally unearthed, in 1971 and was restored by Stanton Macdonald-Wright (see Macdonald-Wright's account). Russell's explanations of this major work help to explain the basis of Synchromism.

In the Bernheim-Jeune exhibition catalog,[9] Russell dedicated the *Synchromie en bleu violacé* to Mrs. Whitney in order to express his deep appreciation for her generosity. He accompanied the dedication of this painting with a quotation (in French) from Genesis, I, iii-iv: "And God said: 'let there be light.' And there was light. And God saw that it was good; and God divided the light from the darkness." Writing to Mrs. Whitney in December 1913, Russell explained that this painting was a "Synchromie to light." Not only did he dedicate this major painting to Mrs. Whitney, but he sent to her in New York most of the pictures from the Bernheim-Jeune exhibition to offer as "a humble gift" those that she might accept; Stanton Macdonald-Wright was to come and take away the remainder. Russell had sold only one work in the Bernheim-Jeune show and Mrs. Whitney chose not to accept any for herself—not even the *Synchromie en bleu violacé* about which he earnestly explained:

> The big canvas which I took the liberty of dedicating to you is the heart of my development and I consider that it belongs to you—it has haunted me for years and was what I wanted to see you about last fall. I hope you like it or come to like it for otherwise I shall be obliged to beg your pardon for the dedicace. Am enclosing a little analysis of the big synchromie which you may care to look at after you have seen the original.

Russell titled the little booklet that he constructed to send to Mrs. Whitney *Harmonic Analysis of the Big Synchromie in Blue-Violacé.* On each tiny page he either carefully illustrated a principle of his design with a sketch or explained an abstract concept in words. Mrs. Whitney did save this little document and another letter that he wrote the following day to explain "why the big picture was a synchromie to light." Russell wrote:

> In my effort to organize a rhythmic ensemble with the simplest elements of light I could not help but have as a result an artistic synthese of the motion experienced by the first eye that opened on this world or varied color and light that we all are so familiar with and which has as basis, as far as we humans are concerned, the spectrum and not the yellow white disk of the sun.

Russell's evolution since the days in 1910 when he had painted still lifes after Cezanne's *Apples,* ca. 1873-77, (borrowed from the collection of Leo and Gertrude

6.
Morgan Russell to Gertrude Vanderbilt Whitney, unpublished letter of 13 September, 1915. This and other unpublished letters to Mrs. Whitney are in the collection of the Whitney Family, New York. Gertrude Vanderbilt Whitney gave Russell an allowance from 1908 to 1915. This portrait appears in the background of a photograph (of Russell's sculpture in his studio) which he sent to Mrs. Whitney in 1915.

7.
In the collection of Mr. and Mrs. Henry M. Reed, Caldwell, **N.J.**

8.
Willard Huntington Wright, *Modern Painting: Its Tendency and Meaning,* New York, 1915, 297.

9.
Bernheim-Jeune et Cie., *Les Synchromistes Morgan Russell et Stanton Macdonald-Wright,* Paris, 1913.

Stein) was dramatic. He now described his *Synchromie en bleu violacé* as: "the bursting of the central spectrum . . . on one's consciousness" and proclaimed:

> If modern painting is to express anything greater than a few apples or portraits it can only be something of this sort—the modern consciousness demands something profoundly organique. A sort of human being flying thru space pointing at a round white disk can no longer mean "let there be light" to us although it did to the contemporaries of the mightiest genius that ever touched an artist's tool.

Morgan Russell's reference to Michelangelo as the "mightiest genius" is a telling one. In his *Harmonic Analysis* he divulged: "I have always felt the need of imposing on color the same violent twists and spirals that Rubens and Michelangelo etc. imposed on form . . ." In his book *Modern Painting,* Willard Huntington Wright wrote:

> In his *Synchromie en bleu violacé* the composition was very similar to that of the famous Michelangelo Slave whose left arm is raised above the head and whose right hand rests on the breast. The picture contained the same movement as the statue, and had a simpler ordonnance of linear directions; but, save in a general way, it bore no resemblance to the human form.[10]

Wright was, of course, referring to Michelangelo's *Dying Captive* in the Louvre which Russell sketched many times. In these sketches Russell concentrated on the figure's contrapposto, fascinated by the imaginary spiral running through the entire figure. It is this spiral rhythm that Russell borrowed as his means of organizing *Synchromie en bleu violacé* around a principal rhythm.

Russell wrote in his *Harmonic Analysis* that "never in painting has color been composed in the same sense." In his statement in the Bernheim-Jeune exhibition catalog, Russell asserted:

> One often hears painters say that they work on the form first with the hope of using color afterwards. It seemed to me that the opposite method should obtain. In the picture named

above, I have labored uniquely with colors—its rhythms, its contrasts and certain directions motivated by color masses. One will not find there a subject matter in the ordinary sense of the word; its subject is "dark blue," evolving according to the intimate form of my canvas.[11]

Russell, exhibiting another of his monumental abstractions, *Synchromy in Orange: To Form,* created a stir in Paris at the Salon des Indépéndants of 1914. Meanwhile, Stanton Macdonald-Wright had arranged a brief Synchromist exhibition from 2 March to 16 March at the Carroll Galleries in New York, providing many young American artists with their first taste of Synchromism.

At the outbreak of the first World War, Russell chose not to join his compatriots in returning home. He became increasingly isolated as the steady flow of young American artists coming to study abroad drew to an abrupt halt. Macdonald-Wright, who had returned to Paris in April 1914, after arranging the Synchromist exhibition in New York, went to London in August where he lived with his brother for two years before going to live in New York from 1916 to 1918. Russell spent a month in New York in 1916 at the time of his participation in the Forum Exhibition. This was the last Russell saw of Macdonald-Wright until he traveled to Los Angeles in 1931 with the hope of being able to resume working and exhibiting together.

Writing to Macdonald-Wright on 15 April 1924, Russell recalled that he had already ceased to paint Synchromies when he came to New York in 1916. He wrote that he had reached an "impasse in my abstract synchromies" and that he was:

> beginning all over at the beginning in painting of the traditional kind. I quit the former, dabbling only with light instead and pushed vigorously the latter by a renewal of interest for painting, realizing I knew next to nothing about it in practice however much in theory . . ."

At the time, Russell's work had evolved far beyond his first and best abstract Synchromies of 1913-1914, characterized by what he had described, in his essay in the catalog of the Forum Exhibition, as "color rhythms" and "a spiralic plunge into space."[12]

10.
Wright, *Modern Painting,* 299.

11.
Bernheim-Jeune et Cie., *Les Synchromistes,* trans. by Stanton Macdonald-Wright, in *An Exhibition in Memoriam: Morgan Russell,* Rose Fried Gallery, New York, 1952, n.p.

12.
The Forum Exhibition of Modern American Painters, Anderson Galleries, New York, n.p.

Yet, in a letter to Mrs. Whitney dated 7 November 1915, Russell affirmed that he planned "to continue unflinchingly. . . to work out the art that I have given birth to, come what may." Apparently he always intended to return to the abstract Synchromist painting that he had momentarily abandoned.

When Russell wrote to Mrs. Whitney from Paris on 1 November 1916, he mentioned that his most recent works were landscapes. He expressed the desire to travel about France in order to see different sites and to refresh his imagination. After such travels, Russell expected that he would then be able to "retire again to studio-land and do spontaneously a few large conceptions that are sure to arise in my imagination." Perhaps the experience in New York had suggested to Russell this more conservative direction, leading him to work from nature once again. Of the seventeen "modern" artists participating in the Forum Exhibition, only he, Macdonald-Wright, Dasburg, Hartley, and Dove showed abstract paintings without recognizable subject matter.

In a letter of 12 August 1917, written from the Alpes Maritime, Russell informed Mrs. Whitney that he had come "south again in order to get as much work done as possible" in the sunny weather. Since he mentioned his work on a series of nudes, he had obviously postponed further his return to abstract Synchromies. On 28 September 1918, Russell married Emilie Francesconi in Nice. They settled in the south of France, where Russell continued to paint landscapes, nudes, and, by 1921, themes from classical mythology.

In the catalog of his Paris exhibition of 1923 at Galerie La Licorne, five *Eidos (themes-synchromatiques) pour une Synchromie à la Vue* are listed. In resuming his abstract Synchromist paintings in early 1922, Russell chose to call this series "Eidos", after the Greek word meaning shape or form. It is interesting that these "Eidos" paintings were themes or studies for a larger, never executed *Synchromy to Vision,* for Russell claimed that he had given up the "vivid color work" in his abstract Synchromies by the summer of 1915 due to eye strain.

The colors of these later Synchromies are more muted. While in his first abstract Synchromies Russell often used the basic hues of the spectrum, the predominant colors in the "Eidos" series are typically raised or lowered in value. Another noticeable development in the "Eidos" paintings and other works after the spring of 1914 is the illusion of a vast blue or empty space receding behind the predominant floating shapes of color to the edges of the frame, letting the color properties alone give the illusion of recession and projection.

In a note in the Galerie La Licorne catalog, Russell attempted to explain the "Eidos" pictures:

> Each Eidos represents the unity of impressions that remain with you after having seen their details unroll on a luminous screen or in the air itself after a display of fireworks. . . the fireworks, which already filled with wonder, rose to the power of a sublime art—then, an art of most modest means, by a luminous screen—arts of an unprecedented power, sleeping, then enlightening reason by divine drunkeness of the senses. . .[13]

In his explanation of the "Eidos" paintings, Russell seems to be referring to his plans for a light machine. Writing to Macdonald-Wright in a letter of 19 October 1922, he expressed his hope that this machine would serve as "a basis for future Synchromies in light" and he asserted: "even if I'm to be obliged to do them only on canvas I'm going along at it, for I'm passionately interested in it and have confidence in its future."

Unfortunately, Russell was never in a financially secure enough position to fully realize these plans. At this time, he lived in the country without electricity and could not even afford to purchase batteries for his machine. He had first conceived of such a machine as early as September 1912. He did some experiments with lights in the winter of 1915-1916 and left extensive notes on his plans.

From 1920 until they were again together in 1931, Russell and Macdonald-Wright discussed their various ideas for a light machine and planned to work together on its realization. On 7 September 1920 Macdonald-Wright first offered to raise the necessary funds to bring him to Los Angeles. Russell responded:

> . . . As to your offer to come I do not hide the fact that it would be a great joy for me to come and work with you in "Lights" as you say. To work at them has been a dream caressed by me for some time, but I had sort of got used to thinking that I would never get the chance to realize this dream. . . .

13.
Exposition Tableaux et Synchromies par Morgan Russell, Galerie La Licorne, Paris, 1923.

Raising the necessary funds for the trip proved more difficult than Macdonald-Wright had imagined. Russell was understandably reluctant to arrive penniless like an immigrant in his own country without an assured source of income.

About 1923, Macdonald-Wright wrote to Russell that he had invented a machine but did not "intend to attempt anything until you are on hand to work at it also." He stressed the necessity of an instrument of "high precision, expensive mechanics, special lenses and of course motor generators and electricity." Russell responded:

> ...I didn't quite understand things you said of your machine. You asked of mine—that makes me laugh—mine! Well, have one, but don't call it anything but a muddle of paper, electric lights and paints, and yet I get remarkable artistic effects and emotions of it on a rudimentary scale— ...the important thing is to get into and arouse the senses of our own species. Get it over on men, not as art necessarily, but as intoxication, as ivresse in spite of ourselves....

Morgan Russell continued to paint occasional Synchromies of the "Eidos" variety until about 1930. During the 1920s, when he suffered from artistic isolation and the resulting poverty, Russell concentrated more and more on a traditional mode of representational painting. Although he produced landscapes, still lifes, and portraits, he considered his figure paintings of the nude to be his most significant output, ranking with his Synchromies in importance. On 10 March 1924, he wrote to Macdonald-Wright:

> I'm slowly evolving for myself a new "canon" of the nude, as it's done out of love and personal inclination, it will not be sterile but fertile, I'm sure. It's one of the elements then of this native art. Another is our Synchromies which I see to be hymns in color and shape, to the infinite. They will be the future expression in art for that innate religiousness in Americans....

Russell's nudes included a variety of mythological figures such as Prometheus, biblical figures such as Job, and various male and female bathers. His nudes found the least acceptance among collectors, putting Russell on the defensive. On 23 December 1924, he wrote to Macdonald-Wright during a stay in Paris: "Of course I don't explain as we used to, about my work—I simply say, 'I like male nudes...'" Commenting on his works in the Salon des Indépendants exhibition of 1923, Russell explained to Macdonald-Wright:

> They are mostly nude compositions—on a subject basis that is unnatural or legendary. This appeals to me and I find it the best scaffolding for big figure work. The originality of subject matter is in my way of seeing nude form—a new angle on the details of nude form from that we have anchored in us, since Greece.

As Russell considered himself to be a "sculpteur manqué," he made clear to Macdonald-Wright the necessity of stressing "solidity" along with "line and color" in painting.[15] In a letter of 10 March 1924, Russell admitted that he still identified as an American artist in spite of his long residence in the tiny French village of Aigremont:

> I've a sort of feeling that after all, what they say of me is true—that I'm American in spite of my years of absorbing culture here. My love of the big—the quantitative (gigantic figures on the landscape) of energy, of male nudes, etc., all point to it, and I'm getting conscious of it as a fact, and proud of it. Of all the men I've met you seem to me alone to have the same rumblings of new energy in your veins and head. It spells to me an American art— not a variant of French art as Spanish and French are variants of Italian Venetian art, but a new and distinctive art....

While focusing on the heroic form of his nude figures, Russell had not forgotten his earlier preoccupation with color. This can be seen in his sumptuous use of color in his floral still life paintings from the 1920s. Russell explained this attitude to Macdonald-Wright:

> ...I am beginning to think that the less color attraction or appeal exists in a figure work, the more expressive becomes the form—I guess that's why I jump to making these colored still life [sic] after doing figure work, as a reaction and contenting of another side of my nature.[16]

Russell was well aware of the necessity of producing saleable works of art. He regularly produced a number of smaller canvases that he shipped unstretched to

---

14.
Morgan Russell to Stanton Macdonald-Wright, unpublished letter of 4 August 1921.

15.
Morgan Russell to Stanton Macdonald-Wright, unpublished letter of 1923.

16.
Morgan Russell to Stanton Macdonald-Wright, unpublished letter of 23 December 1924 from Paris.

Macdonald-Wright in California. The latter managed to sell these to his friends and acquaintances, often for as little as $25, a meaningful sum for the impoverished Russell. After a small exhibition in Paris in January 1925, Russell complained to Macdonald-Wright:

> . . . it's certainly disheartening to entertain vast ambitious projects in one's art, to have spent one's youth attaining to a certain power therein and then be obliged to fritter the whole away trying to sell the pictures one does with the lesser powers of one's talent—and hardly having the wherewithal to feel exalted and paint for oneself the works this puny age doesn't care for. There are moments when I almost feel a revolt. . . .[17]

Russell finally traveled to Los Angeles in July 1931. In the *Los Angeles Times*, Arthur Millier wrote that the Synchromists were at last reunited.[18] This reunion after fifteen years was not to last, however. To reduce expenses Russell had come without his wife; he did not choose to remain. Russell lived in California until June 1932, and the two Synchromists exhibited together in San Francisco and Los Angeles. Russell taught at the Chouinard School of Art and lectured elsewhere in Los Angeles and San Francisco.

Russell and Macdonald-Wright were heralded as "two of the most important living American artists" and their exhibition at the New Stendahl Galleries in Los Angeles was described as "a feast of painting" and "the major exhibit of the season."[19] Russell was generously described as "an oil painter. . . of the tribe of Rembrandt"; his nudes were called "very grand paintings."[20]

Their youthful dreams of fame and fortune were not to be realized. Writing from France in 1930, Russell had expressed to Macdonald-Wright his confidence and admiration for him:

> I have known but one American artist, you! —besides myself perhaps, who has learned the one thing outside of craft practices that Paris can give of value to artists. In other words all foreigners who come to France copy her latest fashions. But French artists create new fashions. Whether they be Americans, Japanese, Swedes, or Esquimaux, they all copy and ape. Incredible, they can't just get the real spirit of Paris, which

is independence and personal growth, reacting not against the old masters, but against the latest advanced fashions.[21]

Yet the two were never again to relive the excitement of the initial Synchromist epoch.

Russell, like other American artists who experimented with pure abstraction in Europe before the first World War, experienced a struggle to maintain his avantgarde instincts during the next decades. Russell had been a member of the Paris art world at its most exciting moment and he later realized the strength of his youthful endeavors. Writing to Macdonald-Wright on 10 October 1925, Russell exclaimed that "my abstract Synchromies . . . are probably the one completely original contribution I'll ever make to an art and more important than all that, they correspond exactly to me mentally."

It was also in 1925 that Russell had discussed with his friend the poet Blaise Cendrars a proposal for a Synchromist ballet to be performed by the Ballet Suédois. When he wrote to his American colleague telling him of Cendrars, he proposed that Macdonald-Wright create a film as a *Synchromist Overtoure* for the ballet:

> His taste and work is [*sic*] very modern and he is one of the few who don't [*sic*] understand why I didn't persevere in painting Synchromies . . . Of course, I've never considered a Synchromist ballet—but at once saw how it could be done and encouraged by his enthusiasm. Now, as you know—I don't wish to noisily resurrect Synchromism with you out of it, any more than you do, by leaving me out in U.S. . . .[22]

The ballet project, like the light machine, was never to be realized.

Morgan Russell and Stanton Macdonald-Wright were privileged to have been in the eye of the avant-garde storm in Paris of 1913. Their deserved notoriety as the co-founders of Synchromism was short-lived. The recovery of Russell's *Synchromie en bleu violacé,* the first and his favorite purely abstract Synchromist painting, is reason to reconsider not only his entire oeuvre but also the Synchromist movement. It is fitting to do so by looking at a group of paintings collected by Russell's close friend and collaborator. Rarely do two creative individuals find such rapport as did Morgan Russell and Stanton Macdonald-Wright.

17.
Morgan Russell to Stanton Macdonald-Wright, unpublished letter of 4 February 1925, from Paris.
18.
A. M. [Arthur Millier], "Synchromists Reunited," *Los Angeles Times,* 19 July 1931.
19.
Arthur Millier, "Wright and Russell Give Season's Major Exhibit," *Los Angeles Times,* 10 January 1932, 16.

20.
Millier, "Wright and Russell," 16.
21.
Morgan Russell to Stanton Macdonald-Wright, unpublished letter of 7 January 1930, from Paris.
22.
Morgan Russell to Stanton Macdonald-Wright, unpublished, undated letter of 1925. Letters from Blaise Cendrars to Morgan Russell discussing the ballet proposal also exist.

Morgan Russell Chronology

Compiled by Gail Levin

1886 25 January—Born in New York City, son of Miner
Antoinette and Charles Jean Russell.

1906 Studied painting in New York with Robert Henri.
Studied sculpture in New York at the Art Students
League with James Earle Fraser.
Spring—First trip abroad to Paris and Italy (to fall).

1907 Spring and summer abroad.

1908 Began receiving a monthly allowance from
Gertrude Vanderbilt Whitney which continued until
1 January 1916.
Met Leo and Gertrude Stein in Paris and through them
Matisse and Picasso. Met Rodin
Interested in painting of Claude Monet, whom he
called a "master of light."

1909 Spring—Settled in Paris. Did not return to the United
States until 1916.
Joined in Paris by Andrew Dasburg who remained
until 1910. They borrowed Leo Stein's Cézanne still
life (*Apples*, ca. 1873-77) and painted works directly
inspired by it.
Exhibited in the Salon d'Automne, Paris.

1910 Exhibited *Bathers* in the Salon d'Automne, Paris.

1911 Began to attend the classes of Ernest Percyval
Tudor-Hart (1873-1954).
Met Stanton Macdonald-Wright.

1912 Salon des Indépendants, Paris.
Began to paint Synchromies.
September—first conceived of a light machine.

1913 Armory Show, New York, 17 February-15 March.
Included *Capucines*, 1912.
Salon des Indépendants, Paris, exhibited his first
Synchromist painting *Synchromie en Vert*.
June—*Ausstellung Der Synchromisten*, first Synchromist
exhibition at Der Neue Kunstsalon, Munich; included
sixteen works by Russell.
27 October-8 November, *Les Synchromistes Morgan
Russell et Stanton Macdonald-Wright*, Bernheim-Jeune
Gallery, Paris; included first abstract Synchromy.

1914 Salon des Indépendants, Paris, exhibited *Synchromie à
la Forme: Orange*, 1913-1914.
2-16 March—*Exhibition of Synchromist Paintings by
Morgan Russell and Stanton Macdonald-Wright* at the
Carroll Galleries, New York.
Summer—traveled in Italy and painted Synchromies.

1915 14-18 March—*Comité de Defense des Professions Liberales*
at the Galerie Chaine et Simonson, Paris.

1916 Traveled to New York at the occasion of his inclusion in
the Forum Exhibition, Anderson Galleries, New York,
13-25 March. Remained for one month, returned to
live in France until 1931.
Stopped painting Synchromies until 1922; worked on
light machine.

1917 Living in Le Cannet, Alpes Maritimes, near Cannes,
France.

1918 Nice—Amedeo Modigliani and Russell painted
portraits of each other.
Moved in Midi.
28 September—Married Emilie Francesconi
(1889-1938).

1919 28 January-12 February—*Le Peintre Morgan Russell*,
exhibition at the Galerie B. Weill, Paris.
April—Group exhibition at La Galerie Branger;
exhibited Paris scenes.
23 July-30 September—Group exhibition at Galerie
d'Art des Editions G. Crès et Cie., Paris.
August—*Exhibition of French Art 1914-1919*, Mansard
Gallery, London, showed three works.
5-20 November—*Inauguration de la Librarie Artistique
Exposition de Noir et Blanc*; included in this drawing
exhibition with Derain, Dufy, Matisse, Picasso,
and others.

1920 January—Salon des Indépendants—exhibited *Achille
et Briséis*.
September—Exhibition at the Galerie Chéron, Paris.

1921 Salon des Indépendants; included *Hercules
Vainqueur* and *Les Dieux S'amusent*.
April—Group exhibition in *Café du Parnasse*,
Paris.
10-31 October—Group exhibition at Galerie
Lucien Vogel, Paris.
Settled in Aigremont.

1922 Salon des Indépendants; included three
works by Russell (*Portrait du Peintre, Danae*, and
Job et son Dieu).
Painted Synchromies of the *Eidos* series.

1923 4-17 May—*Exposition Tableaux et Synchromies Par
Morgan Russell* at Galerie La Licorne, Paris;
included sixty works.
Salon des Indépendants, Paris (*Portrait de la
Famille Sol, Le Jugement de Paris, Les Genies
Joyeux*, and *Landscape*).

1924 Salon des Indépendants, Paris.

1925 January—Galerie Marguerite Henry, Paris.
Salon des Indépendants.
Discussions with poet Blaise Cendrars about
collaborating on a Synchromist ballet for the
Ballet Suédois.
27 November 1925-31 January 1926—
Participated in the *First Pan-American Exhibition
of Oil Paintings* at the Los Angeles County
Museum, exhibited *The Bathers*.

1927 February—*Synchromism* exhibition of twenty-two
works with those of Stanton Macdonald-Wright
at the Los Angeles County Museum.
June—*Synchromism,* Oakland Art Gallery.

1931 July—To California with the help of Stanton
Macdonald-Wright.
5 November-5 December—Exhibition with
Stanton Macdonald-Wright at the California
Palace of the Legion of Honor, San Francisco.
6 November—Lecture on "Ancient and Modern
Art."

1932 Living in Hollywood.
4-23 January—Exhibition of works by Stanton
Macdonald-Wright and Morgan Russell at the
New Stendahl Art Galleries, Los Angeles.
9 January—Lectured on "Ancient and Modern
Art" at New Stendahl Galleries.
16 January—Lectured on "Latin Versus Nordic
Races in the Plastic Arts."
February—*Paintings by Stanton Macdonald-Wright
and Morgan Russell,* Los Angeles County
Museum; twenty-nine works by Russell.
Taught classes in still life painting at the
Chouinard School of Art, Los Angeles.
7-9 April—Pacific Art Association School
Exhibit, Chouinard School of Art.
17 June—Returned to Aigremont, France, via
Antwerp aboard Hamburg American Line's *M.S.
San Francisco.*

1933- Spent winters in Rome.
1935

1936 Moved to Burgundy.

1938 Death of Russell's wife.

1942 *An Exhibition of Fifteen Paintings by Stanton
Macdonald-Wright and a Small Group of Paintings
by Morgan Russell,* New Stendahl Galleries,
Los Angeles, 23 April-16 May.

1946 Moved to the United States, lived in Broomall,
Pennsylvania.
Converted to Catholicism.
9 April-19 May—included in *Pioneers of Modern
Art in America,* Whitney Museum of American
Art, New York.

1950 20 November-30 December—*Three American
Pioneers of Abstract Art,* Rose Fried Gallery,
New York.

1951 *Abstract Painting and Sculpture in America,*
Museum of Modern Art, New York.

1953 29 May—Death of Morgan Russell at home of
son-in-law, A. Atwater Kent Jr., Broomall,
Pennsylvania.

verso 1.
Portrait of a Lady (Emilie Francesconi,
the artist's future wife), 1915

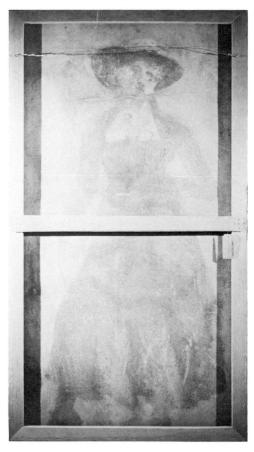

recto 1.
  Untitled (Synchromist Nude), 1912-13

3.
Untitled (Synchromy), ca. 1914?

5.
Eidos #12 (Homage to Einstein),
ca. *1922*

2.
Synchromie en bleu violacé (Synchromy in Blue-Violet), 1913

23

6.
Untitled (Still Life, Flowers),
ca. 1923-25?

7.
Prometheus(?), early 1920s?

10.
Untitled (Male Torso), 1928

14.
Untitled (Male Torso), ca. 1920s

4.
Géant Bouoleeuse? (Inflated Giant?),
1920

11.
Baigneuse (Bather), ca. 1929-30

12.
Siesta, 1920s?

13.
Untitled (Chair), ca. 1920s?

15.
Piscine, 1933

Checklist
Morgan Russell: Unknown Paintings

All works in the exhibition are by Morgan Russell
Dimensions: height x width

1.
recto: *Untitled (Synchromist Nude)*, 1912-13
verso: *Portrait of a Lady* (Emilie Francesconi,
      the artist's future wife), 1915
      Oil on canvas
      67¼ x 37 in. (170.8 x 94 cm.)
      Mrs. Stanton Macdonald-Wright,
        Los Angeles

2.
Synchromie en bleu violacé (Synchromy in Blue-Violet), 1913
Oil on canvas
10 ft. 4 in. x 7 ft. 6 in. (315 x 228.6 cm.)
Mrs. Stanton Macdonald-Wright, Los Angeles

3.
Untitled (Synchromy), ca. 1914?
Oil on canvas
16 x 13⅛ in. (40.6 x 33.3 cm.)
Mrs. Stanton Macdonald-Wright, Los Angeles

4.
Géant Bouoleeuse? (Inflated Giant?), 1920
Oil on canvas
18¼ x 15½ in. (46.4 x 39.4 cm.)
Mrs. Stanton Macdonald-Wright, Los Angeles

5.
Eidos #12 (Homage to Einstein), ca. 1922
Oil on canvas mounted on panel
16 x 10 in. (40.6 x 25.4 cm.)
Mrs. Stanton Macdonald-Wright, Los Angeles

6.
Untitled (Still Life, Flowers), ca. 1923-25?
Oil on canvas
20 x 15 in. (50.8 x 38.1 cm.)
Mrs. Stanton Macdonald-Wright, Los Angeles

7.
Prometheus(?), early 1920s?
Oil on cardboard
23½ x 19½ in. (59.7 x 49.5 cm.)
Mrs. Stanton Macdonald-Wright, Los Angeles

8.
Untitled (Two Figures), early 1920s?
Oil on cardboard
23½ x 19½ in. (59.7 x 49.5 cm.)
Mrs. Stanton Macdonald-Wright, Los Angeles

9.
Untitled (Two Bathers), 1925?
Oil on canvas
20½ x 19¾ in. (52.1 x 50.2 cm.)
Mrs. Stanton Macdonald-Wright, Los Angeles

10.
Untitled (Male Torso), 1928
Oil on canvas
40 x 32 in. (101.6 x 81.3 cm.)
Mrs. Stanton Macdonald-Wright, Los Angeles

11.
Baigneuse (Bather), ca. 1929-30
Oil on canvas
43 x 39½ in. (109.2 x 100.3 cm.)
Mrs. Stanton Macdonald-Wright, Los Angeles

12.
Siesta, 1920s?
Oil on cotton
45 x 57½ in. (114.3 x 146.1 cm.)
Mrs. Stanton Macdonald-Wright, Los Angeles

13.
Untitled (Chair), ca. 1920s?
Oil on canvas
40 x 32 in. (101.6 x 81.3 cm.)
Mrs. Stanton Macdonald-Wright, Los Angeles

14.
Untitled (Male Torso), ca. 1920s
Oil on canvas
14¾ x 18 in. (37.5 x 45.7 cm.)
Mrs. Stanton Macdonald-Wright, Los Angeles

15.
Piscine, 1933
Oil on canvas
36 x 43 in. (91.4 x 109.2 cm.)
Los Angeles County Museum of Art
Gift of Stanton Macdonald-Wright

Photograph Credits:

Los Angeles County Museum of Art: 2, 15.
Randy Sprout: 1, 3, 4, 6, 7, 10, 11, 12, 13, 14.
William B. Tracy: 5.
Jed Wilcox: illus. p. 12.

2.

Dynaton Revisited

It has been a singular pleasure to work with artists Gordon Onslow Ford and Lee Mullican in re-creating the years of their intimate association and their connection with the late Wolfgang Paalen in the Dynaton movement. At our request both artists wrote the moving and enlightening essays about that special movement twenty-five years ago when they worked closely together in the Bay Area.

We regret the death, while preparing this commemorative exhibition, of Jacqueline Johnson, Gordon Onslow Ford's wife of thirty-seven years and a marvelously gifted writer who contributed a great deal to the Dynaton sensibility. By all accounts she was a figure whose memory remains truly cherished. We admire and appreciate Gordon Onslow Ford's brave and generous spirit throughout this difficult period.

Onslow Ford's retrospective exhibition, featuring new work, opens at the Oakland Art Museum in Spring 1977 and will travel throughout the country. Mullican's new paintings have not been exhibited publicly in this decade; we expect them to create an exceptional impact when we present them at LACMA. The time for a reassessment of Wolfgang Paalen's historic achievement and an account of his remarkable life and tragic early death in Mexico in 1959 is also at hand.

Sylvia Fink teaches at Arizona State University, where she wrote her dissertation on the Dynaton artists; for this publication she has prepared a new manuscript on the movement.

M. T.

Apartment of Gordon Onslow Ford and
his wife Jacqueline Johnson, late 1940s.
The *Dynaton* group was formed there.
Standing, left to right: Lee Mullican and
Gordon Onslow Ford. Seated, left to
right: Jacqueline Johnson and Luchita
Paalen (née Hurtado).

The Dynation: Three Artists with Similar Ideas— Lee Mullican, Gordon Onslow Ford, Wolfgang Paalen

Sylvia Fink

In the late 1940s Gordon Onslow Ford and Wolfgang Paalen were living in the San Francisco area where they became acquainted with Lee Mullican. Mullican and Onslow Ford describe elsewhere in this catalog how it came to pass that the three wrote a manifesto and had an exhibition. This exhibition, known as *Dynaton,* was accompanied by a publication *Dynaton 1951.*

Surrealism was a common denominator in the background of all three artists. The Surrealists had used automatic methods of producing art. While an intuitive approach remained important to the Dynaton artists, it was not as an end product itself, but rather raw material which might suggest new possibilities.

Paalen's reputation was established with his one-man exhibiton in 1936 at the Galerie Pierre, Paris. He was an active participant in the Surrealist group and showed in some of the more notable exhibitions.[1] He also helped organize the *Exposition Internationale de Surréalisme,* Paris, in 1938, the same year Onslow Ford joined the Surrealists.

Onslow Ford spent the summer of 1938 in Brittany painting with Matta. He abandoned working directly from nature; rather in these new works nature appeared obliquely in a series of automatic drawings. Onslow Ford returned to England in 1939, where he worked as an assistant editor on the Surrealist-oriented publication *London Bulletin.* An article he wrote for this magazine, "The Painter Looks Within Himself," contained some of the ideas he later presented to young artists two years later when he lectured at the New School for Social Research in New York.

Onslow Ford came to New York at the invitation of the Society for the Preservation of European Culture and quickly became a force in the New York art scene. His lectures promoted the idea "...that an exploitation of

the possibilities of automatism was the most fruitful direction in which the Surrealists could venture."[2] At Onslow Ford's request, a series of exhibitions was arranged to accompany his lecture. These exhibitions included not only his work, but that of Arp, Brauner, de Chirico, Delvaux, Domiquez, Ernst, Frances, Hayter, Magritte, Matta, Miró, Moore, Paalen, Seligmann, and Tanguy.[3]

Before André Breton, the chief theoretician of Surrealism, came to New York in 1941 and assumed the leadership of the Surrealist group, Onslow Ford gathered around him many of the artists disposed to Surrealism.[4] The fact that his native language was English must have served an important role in transmitting the Surrealist ideas to New York artists.

Wolfgang Paalen had been invited to Mexico in 1939 by Diego Rivera and his wife Frieda Kahlo. On the way from Paris to Mexico, he detoured to the west coast of British Columbia and traveled to southern Alaska, enabling him to fulfill a desire he had had for years — to study at the source of what remained of the Indian art of the American northwest coast and to see Canada and Alaska.[5] Paalen's admiration of the native American art was shared by all the Dynaton artists. The year after he arrived in Mexico, Paalen helped organize the International Surrealist exhibition, the first major Surrealist exhibition in Mexico.

Paalen has been credited with the introduction of the "plastic" expression of Surrealism to Mexico. Though Breton had been in Mexico and had talked to Rivera and other Mexican painters, it was Paalen who was instrumental in organizing the exhibition of Surrealist art. He has been called a pioneer in Mexican culture, not only of the Surrealist art, but of abstract art as well. Possibly his presence shook the nationalist

---

1.
His work was included in the following exhibitions:
Exposition Surréaliste d'Objet, Galerie Charles Ratton, Paris 1936; *Fantastic Art, Dada, Surrealism,* Museum of Modern Art, New York 1936; *Exposition Internationale de Surréalisme,* Galerie Beaux Arts, Paris, 1938.
2.
Irving Sandler, *The Triumph of American Painting: A History of Abstract Expressionism* (New York: Praeger, 1970), 43.
3.
Irving Sandler, "Dada, Surrealism and Their Heritage: 2. The Surrealist Emerges in New York," *Artforum,* VI (May 1968), 25-26.
4.
Sandler, "Dada, Surrealism," 26.
5.
Leonor Morales Garcia, *Wolfgang Paalen, Introductor del Surrealismó en México* (Unpublished master's thesis, Universidad Iberoamericano, Mexico City, 1965), 34.

structure of Mexican painting and that it was under his influence that Mexico entered the international art arena.[6]

In 1940, on a trip to New York, Paalen had his first one-man exhibition in the United States at the Julien Levy Gallery. It was to be his last Surrealist presentation before he left the group. In Mexico he founded the magazine *Dyn*. The first issue appeared in 1942 and contained his official "Farewell to Surrealism." Onslow Ford left the Surrealist group the following year.

Dyn was one of the most avant-garde art reviews that appeared during World War II. It not only circulated illustrations of some of the more established artists, such as Picasso, Braque, Chagall, Matta, and Moore, but also included writings and some of the earliest illustrations of young New York artists such as Baziotes, Motherwell, and Pollock. Articles were presented on the Indian arts of the Americas, as well as writings about the philosophy of art. Though printed in Mexico, it was written in French and English and was available in the United States. The fact that the magazine became self-supporting attests to its success. Artists who have recognized its influence include Mullican and Diebenkorn.[7]

Paalen's paintings, which emerged from the philosophy he expounded in *Dyn*, were reproduced in the magazine and seen in one-man exhibitions at Ines Amor's gallery in Mexico and Peggy Guggenheim's Art of This Century Gallery in New York. Paalen shared a view with some of the New York artists that automatism was only a raw material for the artist and not a finished product itself. His vehemently brushed, large oil paintings contained characteristics similar to those which would later appear in the work of many New York artists.

Motherwell worked with Paalen during the fall and early winter of 1941.[8] He translated Paalen's article, "The New Image," into English, and it was published in the first issue of *Dyn* in both French and English. Motherwell has stated that their relationship was based on an exchange of information. Paalen gave him "a great deal of information about the origins and nature of Surrealism," and Motherwell gave Paalen "equally factual information about contemporary philosophy in the English-speaking world." Motherwell commented,

"I began painting full-time at precisely, but by coincidence, the same moment that I met Paalen. What we did do, as then-isolated Western intellectuals in Mexico, was to encourage each other in our various aspirations and with our various bits of knowledge and intuitions." He prefers to think "our [Paalen, Matta, Onslow Ford, and Motherwell] joint enthusiasms were based on possibilities that Surrealism suggested to us, and which we transformed in our various ways according to our talents and temperaments."[9]

In 1945, Paalen's book *Form and Sense*, which contained a reprinting of selections of his article from *Dyn*, was published in the United States. The following year Gustav Regler published his monograph *Wolfgang Paalen*. In 1946, Paalen and Onslow Ford had one-man exhibitions of their current work in New York at the Karl Nierendorf Gallery.

Onslow Ford and his wife, Jacqueline Johnson, arrived in Mexico two years after Paalen. The friendship between the two men ripened and the Onslow Fords both contributed to the last issue of *Dyn*.

The Onslow Fords established their home in a vacant mill located on the edge of a village inhabited by Tarascan Indians. Here Onslow Ford became fascinated with Indian art and culture. He has said, "...The Indians and their ancient art have been to me as Negro art was to the Cubists: a formal inspiration."[10] They lived in Mexico for six years; in 1947 they moved to the San Francisco area. In the late 1940s Paalen and Mullican were also in San Francisco.

Lee Mullican was the youngest of the three artists. During World War II he served as a topographic draftsman in the Corps of Army Engineers. Part of his duties involved freehand drawing of maps from aerial photographs. This bird's-eye view of the landscape fascinated him and was to be influential. While stationed in Hawaii he discovered a copy of *Dyn*. The writings and reproductions in this magazine were a revelation in the sense that he felt something of significance was continuing in modern art even during the disaster of the War. He subsequently saw future issues of *Dyn*, as well as Paalen's book *Form and Sense*.

During the War, Mullican made drawings that were influenced by Surrealism; and he was attracted simultaneously to the works of Paul Klee. Traces of this

6.
García, *Paalen*, 80-81.
7.
Frederick Wight, "Diebenkorn, Woelffer, Mullican: A Discussion," *Artforum*, (April 1963), 26.
8.
Frank O'Hara, *Robert Motherwell* (New York: Museum of Modern Art, 1965), 74
9.
Copy of a letter written by Robert Motherwell, which was sent by him to the author.

10.
Gordon Onslow Ford, "Paalen the Messenger," *Homage to Wolfgang Paalen* [from a catalog printed on the occasion of an exhibition of Wolfgang Paalen's work] (Mexico City: Museo de Arte Moderno, 1967), 24.

can be seen in the publication *The Gain of Aft,* 1947, which he wrote and illustrated. Between 1946 and 1950, Mullican's work was used to illustrate several publications, including Glen Coffield's book *The Night is Where You Fly,* 1949; and James Broughton's *Musical Chairs: A Songbook for Anxious Children,* 1950.

Paalen and Onslow Ford had one-man exhibitions at the San Francisco Museum of Art in 1948. In conjunction with Onslow Ford's show, the Museum published his book *Toward a New Subject in Painting,* which contained the idea that the great adventure was "man himself, and the greatest unknown, the human mind." For Onslow Ford the mind was of primary importance, as it sustained that inner world which furnished him with subject matter.

The following year the Museum mounted a one-man exhibition of Mullican's work; Paalen wrote a forward for the catalog, which was reprinted in 1950 for the catalog of Mullican's first New York exhibition at Willard Gallery.

During this period visits and the interchange of ideas led the three artists to realize that they were working toward similar objectives. In 1950 they exhibited at the Stanford University Art Gallery; the show was accompanied by lectures by Sybil Moholy-Nagy, Paalen, and Onslow Ford. In January of the following year the *Dynaton* exhibition was held at the San Francisco Museum of Art. In addition to the artists' paintings and sculptures, the show contained a gallery called the "Ancestor Room" which was filled with works collected by the three — Pre-Columbian, Northwest Coast Indian, and Pacific Islands art.

Dynaton 1951, which was published in conjunction with the exhibition, contained writings by Paalen and Jacqueline Johnson. Johnson described the art as "an insight that emerges more clear, more touching, when it surprises with its revelation even the man who makes it. So that the method of these paintings may be properly called *auto-plastic.*"[11]

Paalen wrote of a philosophy of the possible. He spoke of a *"dynatic* continuum" — *dynatic,* not identical with, but derived from the Greek *tó dynatón*: the possible. In his definition, "the Dynaton is a limitless continuum, in which all forms of reality are potentially implicit."[12] Paalen called their work Meta-plastic, and stated: "The unconscious urge for a self-transcending understanding of the world had become conscious in a meta-plastic vision. Meta-plastic painting is a sort of active meditation which leads to a new concept of reality. This concept assumes that the imponderable is as important as the measurable."[13]

An intuitive approach to art remained important for the Dynaton artists and allowed them to probe the inner mind for subject matter. The space as well as the subject matter of Dynaton paintings is conceptual, not perceptual. It is not the static space associated with traditional perspective painting. The canvases are compositions of lines and dashes of color, which ambiguously change from background to foreground and appear to shift into different forms and patterns.

As a movement, Dynaton had a brief life. Mullican, Onslow Ford, and Paalen soon moved away from San Francisco, and what had existed as a group was disbanded. The ideas which they had shared, however, remain, transmitted through catalogs, photographs, documentation, writings, and — most important — the paintings and sculptures themselves.

11.
Jacqueline Johnson et al., *Dynaton 1951* (San Francisco: The San Francisco Museum of Art, 1951), 40.

12.
Johnson et. al., *Dynaton 1951,* 22.

13.
Johnson et. al., *Dynaton 1951,* 11.

Thoughts on the Dynaton, 1976

Lee Mullican

The initial essay in the first issue of the magazine *Dyn*, 1942, is called "The New Image." With the opening sentence Paalen proclaims his role: "When the intellectual habits of his culture become radically changed the artist must concern himself with theories whether he wants to or not."

Dyn gave Paalen a voice for these *theories* and thoughts on Art, Archaeology, and Science. After the magazine ceased publication it was natural for this remarkable man to create *The Dynaton* as a forum where he could once more publish and present ideas, as well as correlate and enunciate early concepts and feelings that furthered his proclamation of *The Possible*. It was Paalen then who brought *The Dynaton* into being. Now, twenty-five years later, it is once again in view. Paalen was the commander—precise, polite, erudite; his fingers electric, a mind in touch with the cosmos. He was there, spatial, transparent, *aware*, revealing for us maps, traces of ancestral caves, cities to come. With the Dynaton an important aspect of the *Space Age* began. Now, 1976, Los Angeles, that *Starship* once again is to be seen, remembered.

We were three painters. Separately, we had each been given one-man shows at the San Francisco Museum of Art, and as we met and observed each other's work we began a natural bridge that would support a joint manifestation—something beyond another exhibition. There would be a catalog, statements of position; it was important to tell who we were, predict where we were going. How fortunate that Jacqueline Johnson was willing to join us and *Take a Sight* with her catalog essay. We were locating ourselves in that year, 1951.

Our passage was planned. There were talks and discussions over the most elegant of dinners; toasts of the finest wines in select restaurants of San Francisco and Mexico City. I guess I mostly listened. But there

we were, sensing each other out, politely admiring one another's work. . . . How could it be—that these three from such diverse backgrounds could be picnicking at Teotihuacan where we walked around the Pyramids of the Sun and Moon? At times we were silent, standing in a redwood grove. A kinship grew and it would all happen. But when?

Then one day there was a letter with Paalen quoting from *Alice in Wonderland*. Even though he was Austrian, Paalen knew folktales in every language. "'The time has come,' the walrus said, (to speak of many things. . . .'" He was to speak of *The Dynaton* and form it almost whole. Events in Mexico had placed the time, 1951. The place, San Francisco.

Color plates for the catalog were to be made in Mexico. (My contribution was the wrong format and angrily rejected. I later made color separations in San Francisco for the picture reproduced in the catalog. There was no original. I called it *Cast of the Antilon*. It was printed as *Cast of Antilon*. Much better. The work exists only as a reproduction.)

Once settled in the great Victorian house in Mill Valley, there were walks through the wooded paths of the vast garden. Paalen spoke of "the possible not having to be justified by the known" in more human terms. Here, in Marin County, there was a quiet in nature that we all recognized as vital. I remember Paalen proposing that the skeleton of a whale might help ornament the garden, put among the laurel and fern. When the question was asked, "Where is Paalen?" the answer then could be, "Paalen is not here, he is in the whale."

For myself, an introduction to *The Dynaton* began with the magazine *Dyn*, seen by chance in a library in Hawaii during World War II. As a young painter just out of art school with almost two years at war, feeling inextricably caught up in the Pacific, longing for some contact with a distant, almost forgotten, world of Modern Art, the discovery of avant-garde magazines such as *VVV* and *Dyn* was my grasp of a belief in a future where I felt my convictions of success as an artist would be realized. I wanted to be convinced that a new world of painting and abstract thought would be there. *Dyn* was a major signpost. Another was the name Wolfgang Paalen.

I later discovered that many of the Paalen articles from *Dyn* had been published as a book under the title *Form and Sense*. (From the series *Documents of Modern Art* published by Wittenborn and Company. This has long been unavailable and should have been reprinted two decades ago.) With *Form and Sense* Paalen became a force in International Art. During this time I also saw an article in *Time* magazine; it may have been in the nature of a review of his exhibition at Peggy Guggenheim's Art of This Century Gallery. In any case, there was a quotation, now famous, picked up, spoken around the world, seldom identified with the true source. Paalen put the future of Modern Art into focus when he suggested that, just as the spectator may *question the painting,* in turn, the painting may examine the viewer, and as well ask, "What do *you represent?*"

Later, in 1948, I would see the first exhibition of Paalen's painting. It was a memorable event. I stood in the vortex, surrounded by canvases of Lordly Presences, heavy, somber, almost from a nether world, certainly far from the sunlit fields and refractions of the West I was recognizing in my own paintings. And, indeed, I did shrink in their presence as they most certainly questioned me in a most profound manner. I recognized genius in those heads, figures, personages, pierced by rays of light, Messengers from endless space. It will be an important occasion when a full exhibition of the Paalen paintings of that period can again be re-created. Then, perhaps, once again, we can examine and rediscover a Twenty-First Century Man.

I arrived in San Francisco after the War and began to paint in a clean, vivid, automatic, new way, forgetting the surreal imagery I had toyed with as a student. Abstraction once again challenged me. French Painting was my excitement. San Francisco was a challenge, active — my Paris. I felt the light in the West and remembered the red earth of the Southwest. Some of these canvases were eventually seen by Gordon Onslow Ford and his wife, Jacqueline. In time, we met, and I learned what Surrealism had really been about. It was de Chirico, not Dali.

I was introduced to Paalen and his beautiful wife, Luchita Hurtado, at a memorable dinner party shortly after their first arrival from Mexico. And later I trembled with nervousness as I welcomed these guests into my Russian Hill studio. They had brought gifts of wine and cheese. There were remarks about Navajo rugs and then they looked attentively as I displayed my work. It was only later, as we walked down Green Street for a lunch in North Beach, that I was sure I had made some impression. Paalen said, "If you have your exhibition at the Museum, and I am convinced you will, I will be pleased to write something as an introduction."

I was honored and knew I would have to have a catalog. The exhibition was approved and the catalog was printed by my friend Jack Stauffacher of the Greenwood Press, who would later print *The Dynaton* catalog.

The introduction was *right* and I also used it later in a catalog for my first exhibition at the Willard Gallery in New York City.

Paalen always wanted to clear the air:

> If it were only possible for more people to participate in the incomparable joy of seeing what does not look like anything else. . . .

> Any kind of universal language has to be learned. . . .

> The painter of today who has to say something about a tree *as a painter* will not represent but rather ask: what in the Universe does a tree represent? And if he succeeds in formulating his pictorial meditation, he will achieve a perennial image of the tree as it appears in a human mind, instead of copying the chance image on his retina.

These were sentences pulling my near-blind search into focus. I had been working on pure intuition — with the idea that, "Okay, I will tell you what I am painting after I see what the brush and knife has put on the canvas."

Installation photographs, *Dynaton* exhibition, 1951.

Before and parallel with my association with Paalen was the immediate brotherhood I felt with Gordon. It was easier to talk with this man. I knew what he was saying. One day a smiling Gordon, almost with mischief, like jam on his face, arrived at my studio door with a masterpiece of watercolor in hand (*The Robber and the Rose,* 1944). He was generously suggesting an exchange. He must have known there were things in that painting I should know about (as he had once shut me away in his storeroom, a drink in my hand, his early Surrealist paintings propped up in an array of swimming worlds around me).

The painting of mine selected for the exchange was later reproduced in his book, *Towards a New Subject in Painting.* He needed a title for the little canvas and suggested *The Dust Bowl Amiably.* It was a grin-of-a-title with a nod toward my home state and the poetry of Gertrude Stein. Someone he had known. At the time I was reading and collecting her works.

I was complimented, pleasured, flattered to be included in *Towards a New Subject in Painting.* To be brought into focus along with Miró and Gordon's friends, Matta and Tanguy, was an unexpected triumph. I was honored by this first, new painter-friend. Indeed more, I was welcomed. Every meeting with Gordon and Jacqueline was a revelation of thought, of ideas kindly and graciously introduced. The look, the startled sigh of Jacqueline as she, at whatever time, examined a new painting, was more revealing and meaningful than any words.

The Onslow Ford apartment on Chestnut Street was filled with masterpieces of twentieth century art (see illustration). An oval, Cubist Braque. Several de Chiricos, Picasso, Klee, Ernst, and other Surrealists such as Brauner, Delvaux, and, more importantly, the several Matta drawings and the Paalens. This was a formidable collection, not formed from wealth, but from insight, from action and belief. It was in this rare atmosphere that one had formidable dinners — tea with Duchamp — and there the formal portrait of the Dynaton was decided upon and taken.

With the installation at the San Francisco Museum, creative pleasures resumed. Only the artist knows how to hang his work. There was an immediate conflict with the Museum staff over the installation. Gordon had explicit ideas and in a demand for autonomy we

were eventually taken to Dr. Grace Morley, the director. She gave us free rein and we were then in a position to do with the show as we pleased. There were unorthodox ideas, as the installation photos show. Paintings were positioned in clusters, some high, some low, few on a continuous eye level.

I remember Gordon brandishing a hammer above his head and shouting to the departing crew, "We are going to transform this Museum."

The installation fell into place. I remember tacking up some unframed drawings, cut-outs of colored paper. One of these turned a corner on the pillar where it was placed. It was titled *Angus.*

Even with the installation — it wasn't *the thinkable* but also *the possible.* Exhibition photographs were taken. One was a portrait of the three of us cowering in a corner. The exhibition was also put on color motion-picture film. Now lost. There was a vernissage for friends and Museum members. The catalog was ready. It was there. *The Dynaton.*

As I reminisce on the exhibition I am again to speak of *The Starship.* Had there been video at that time each canvas would have been seen as monitoring other worlds. My *Agawam Triptych* (cat. no. la, b, c.) Paalen's shaped canvas *Meditation.* Gordon's *Gentle Balloons* and *Great Haunts.* Space Voyagers, alert! Moonwalks on the hour. And then, we had our relics on board. Relics of the future. There was a remarkable Onslow Ford painting on stretched hide strung on a shaped iron-rod frame. There was the Dynatic sculpture of Paalen that appeared at the *core* — as mysterious as his *Planetary Face* (cat. no. 9).

I had included several painted, wooden, stick-objects. Paalen could not resist giving them a name. "Call them *Tactile Ecstatics,*" he laughed. I must have said, timidly, "that's a joke," but why not. This was, in a sense, the spirit in which they had been made. I thought of them as playful extensions of my paintings. Temporary, put together with string and glue, perhaps to be destroyed like a Tibetan Ghost Trap at the end of the day, even as I had seen a Navajo Sand Painting brushed away as the sun went down. Few of these constructions have survived. I have reconstructed one for this exhibition (cat. no. 3).

Installation photograph, *Dynaton* exhibition, 1951.

We brought our ancestors with us. Included in the original exhibition was a smaller gallery of cases which we filled with masterpieces of Tribal Art. This section was appropriately called, "The Ancestor Room." (Gordon had delight in suggesting we call it "The Lovelies.") Today one finds that what used to be called *Primitive Art* is now being retitled *Ancestral Art.* We felt those roots. There had been a prophetic Amerindian issue of *Dyn.*

The Museum cases held some of the finest Northwest Coast pieces from the Paalen collection. Pre-Columbian artifacts were offered by the Onslow Fords. I had collected few things but did include a recently acquired Pomo Indian feather basket. Ancestors with their magic and ritual were aboard the Starship. Trailing perhaps, but there.

I believe Paalen's most productive period of significant work and revelation actually occurred before the *Dynaton* show; with many of those works in the exhibition. San Francisco did not offer *The Golden Gate to The Future* we had hoped for. Working there was especially difficult for Paalen. Roots had once again been exposed. In 1959 he sent transparencies of recent paintings, his last. They seemed to be less cosmic, closer, from a garden. But even in the finite there was the infinite. The paintings were lyrical, swarming patches of color that dazzled the surface — frozen. We knew he was fighting faltering ebb of health and spirit.

Gordon and I took personal paths, yet were often spiraling around the same mountain, not too far apart. We both became interested in Zen as Alan Watts appeared. Gordon followed this into calligraphy and eventually his line-circle-dot and *Painting in the Instant.* I skyrocketed into Los Angeles for a new beginning where I could more individually begin to make measurements and deal with those things I had yet to explore. A true vision must be formed carefully.

While Paalen's greatest period was before the *Dynaton,* I believe that Gordon and I later found a maturity that was only hinted at during that time. Gordon found his peace in Inverness [California] where he has remained steadfast and devoted to his pursuit — *The Space Traveler,* early on. He is now moving superbly in his search for the inner being.

Looking back, and I prefer not to, I feel that I have in some way stumbled through; sensed, and with a pure, jazz bravado sought the creation with a fresh spirit. I hope so. Yet, I have always been in contact with that *New Subject;* still, *The Dynaton,* floating in my memory as a softened sun, welcomed back, still reflecting off of the Agawam.

The imponderable is as important as the measurable.

Standing, left to right: Gordon Onslow Ford, Lee Mullican, and Jacqueline Johnson. Seated, left to right: Luchita Paalen and Wolfgang Paalen. The wooden object over the mirror is one of Mullican's "Tactile Ecstatics."

Reflections on the Dynaton Exhibition
25 Years Later

Gordon Onslow Ford

André Breton in his article in *Minotaure* 12-13, 1939, "The Latest Tendencies of Surrealist Painting," announced a new direction. These were reproductions in color of paintings by Giorgio de Chirico, Yves Tanguy, Victor Brauner, Wolfgang Paalen, Matta, and by me.

When the Surrealists gathered during the War in New York City in 1940-41, the split between André Breton and those members of the Surrealist group who in Paris were in favor of adopting policies to which André Breton was opposed, was patched up. With the old guard together again, the young Surrealists found themselves much on their own: Matta was in New York City where he shone like a meteor; Paalen and I were in Mexico in relative isolation from the international art world.

Paalen, Matta, and I were grounded in Surrealism, but each of us made our major contributions at different times and in places in the psyche deeper than had been attained by Surrealist painters before.

Matta gave the first impetus in 1938 when he found a new vision of reality that he called psychological morphology.

Paalen in 1941 revealed with his haunting *Spacial Beings* that space is alive.

In 1951, five months after the opening of the *Dynaton* exhibition, it suddenly became clear to me that the root of art was made up of line, circle, dot elements.

* * * * *

In Paris in the late 1930s Paalen's *Fumage* was a distinguished contribution to automatic surrealist techniques. Paalen treated *Fumage* as a field in which his world, rooted in dream and myth, could be revealed. He used *Fumage* much as Max Ernst used *Frottage* and *Decalcomania*. But it was on this continent that Paalen took off on his own; he was inspired by his trip to the Canadian northwest, the Indian cultures of Mexico, the stimulation of his new interest in science, and the thought of John Dewey.

On this continent Paalen changed from painting romantic subjects such as *Fata Alaska*, 1937, and the *Combat of the Saturnian Princes*, 1938, to painting inner-space beings. They are silent apparitions of other dimensions whose preverbal message is contained in the lines, forms, and colors in which they appear.

Paalen made many original paintings which he could have elaborated such as his unique *Space Unbound*, 1941, in which alternating bands of hot and cold colors forming endless spirals were used to express a vision of an all-embracing space-matter, and *The Silent Ones*, 1946, in which he saw the importance of the calligraphic line in the expression of the inner-worlds in which there are no surfaces and all is visible.

In Paalen's remarkable magazine *Dyn*, published in Mexico (1942-45), profound preoccupations with art and science were awakened. When Paalen came to California he wished to make a synthesis of his ideas, and he set to work on *Dynaton*.

* * * * *

The Surrealist Manifesto of 1924 was the result of years of discussion and exchange in cafés and studios between André Breton and his friends, but Paalen wrote *The Dynaton* on his own mostly in Mill Valley. It was the product of his avid reading, his active imagination, and was put together with an urgency, as if he knew that he did not have much time. The text was not seen by Jacqueline [Johnson], Lee Mullican, or by me until it was finished just before the exhibition opened. Paalen's *The Dynaton* contains potent seeds, but the published version now appears to me to be written to meet a deadline. Had he not died so young, he might well have taken it up again and made changes, clarifications, and expansions. The interruption of his thought and his paintings that led up to the *Dynaton* exhibition was a great loss to the development of modern art.

When Paalen went from California to Paris in 1951, he rejoined old friends who were burdened with the troubles of post-War Europe and had little new to give him. Later he became fascinated with Impressionism. His paintings became the work of a master, rather than those of a pioneer.

*   *   *   *   *

Lee Mullican was the first person of genius that I met on coming to the West coast in 1948. When he appeared on the scene after the long night, the sun came out. His paintings in the *Dynaton* exhibition were automatic, or, as I prefer to say, spontaneous from beginning to end. He did not talk much, and awareness of these paintings takes place so fast that words are left behind; his weightless strokes just happened naturally, one leading to the next, and his arcs swung deep and far. He was a dancing man with toes and fingers marking the golden air. His contribution to the exhibition brought a refreshing and carefree note.

*   *   *   *   *

In 1938 I started to make automatic lines, and I saw that each had a life of its own, without the usual addition of anthropomorphic suggestions or later interpretations. By 1942, in *The Circuit,* I was able to enter an inner-world that had its own reality and that did not resemble any known thing, yet was recognizable to those with an open mind.

Many of my paintings in the *Dynaton* exhibition were in a state of transition from the landscapes of the inner-worlds to deeper worlds where, rather than viewing a painting from outside as a spectator, the painting was entered to become an encompassing experience. My painting *Dwellers in the Clear,* 1945, is divided into zones by straight and curved lines (cat. no. 5). Positions of space-divided matter are represented by black, white, and three blues of different values. Zones of space are divided into dots of two values so that there is an uninterrupted passage from one zone to the next. Two line-beings with auras of color face each other and are in close relation through space. Above there is a Messenger and a guardian moon. Perhaps it could be said that the Muse as the female creative principal who had in previous paintings been dominant is making a gift of power to the male creative princi-

pal who will preside over the next stage of involutim until the male and female join once again later on in the depths. Paintings of this time exist in themselves, but they are also forerunners of the line-circle-dot paintings that were to follow shortly after the *Dynaton* exhibition in 1951.

I did not make any remarks for the *Dynaton* catalog. In 1948 I had had a retrospective at the San Francisco Museum of Art for which I wrote a small book, *Towards a New Subject in Painting,* in which the paintings of Wolfgang Paalen and Lee Mullican were included and in which, to the best of my ability at that time, I had briefly suggested a point of view. I was happy that it was the turn of Wolfgang Paalen and Jacqueline to write. Her essay titled, "Taking a Sight," 1951, which, besides referring to painting, also refers to fixing one's position on the earth through observations of the sun, moon, and stars, could have been an alternative title for the exhibition.

*   *   *   *   *

Dynaton was an offspring of Surrealism born into a different state of awareness. By the time of the *Dynaton* exhibition the experiences of the inner-worlds of Wolfgang Paalen, Lee Mullican, and myself had gone beyond periodic insights; we were living them. The different places in those vast expanses in which each of us found himself were more certain, more secure than the dangerous landscapes of Surrealism which alternated between joys and terrors.

The *Dynaton* exhibition appeared in San Francisco on one of Paalen's parabolas that dwelt there at the moment of its turning point, and then dashed off towards the deep black and white.

As pioneer-painters, Wolfgang Paalen, Lee Mullican, and I were strangers to the local art world and with the passage of the years remained so until the last months, when, I am happy to say, there has been among a few an awakening interest.

I am grateful that Maurice Tuchman felt that the time was ripe for a small commemorative exhibition at the Los Angeles County Museum of Art. I hope that it will invite further curiosity and will inspire young painters to work spontaneously and voyage in unexplored places of inner-space, where, in my opinion, the future of modern art lies.

5.
Gordon Onslow Ford
Dwellers In The Clear, 1945

4.
Gordon Onslow Ford
A Present for the Past, 1942

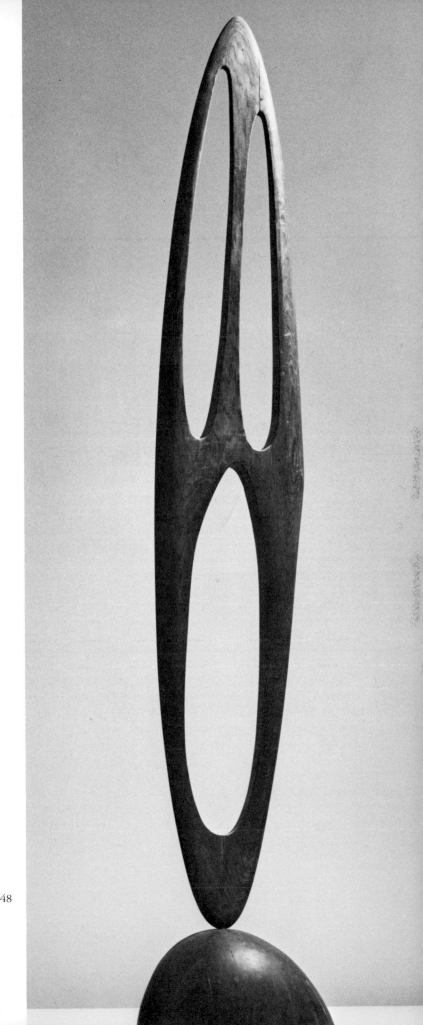

10.
Wolfgang Paalen
Model for a Large Monument, 1948

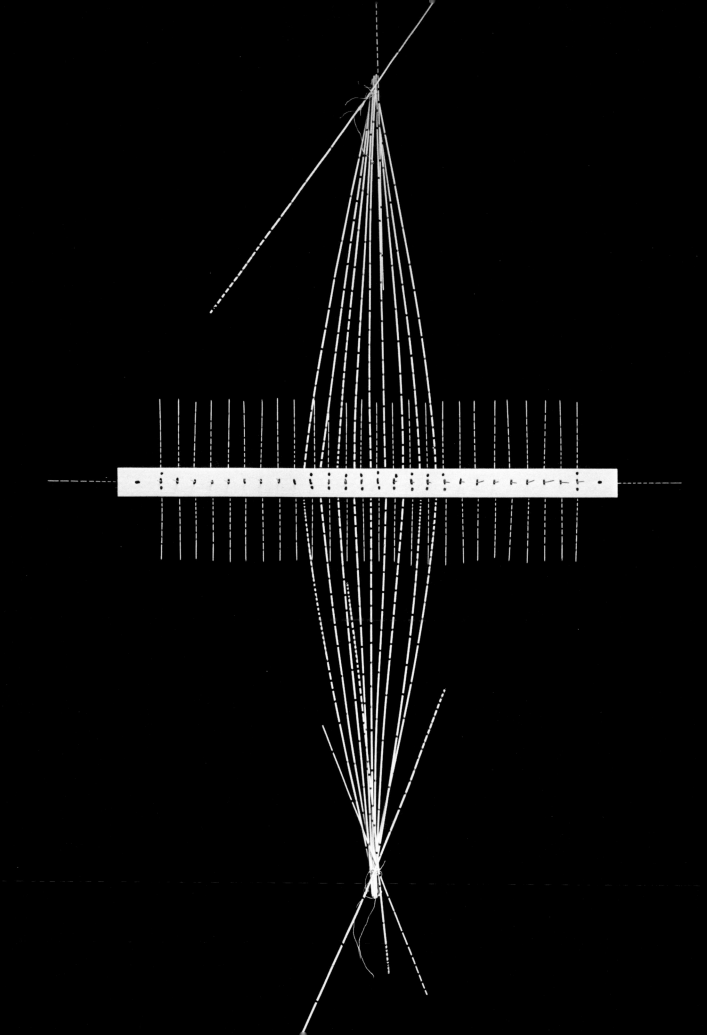

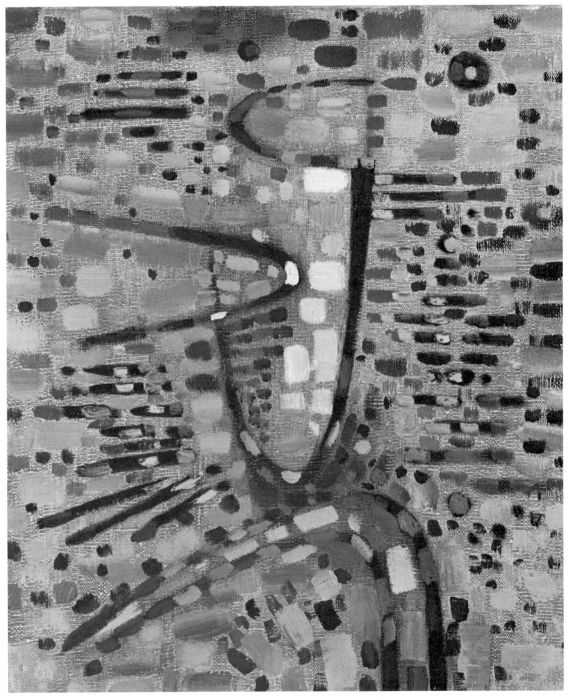

8.
Wolfgang Paalen
Face, ca. 1945

3.
Lee Mullican
Space Scribe (Tactile Ecstatic), 1976
(In the style of the artist's sculptures,
1950-51)

1.
Lee Mullican
Agawam Triptych, 1950
a. Left: *First Quarter*
b. Center: *Oblique of Agawam*
c. Right: *Third Quarter*

Checklist
Dynaton Revisited

Dimensions: height x width x depth

Lee Mullican
Born 1919, Chickasha, Oklahoma
Lives in Santa Monica, California

1.
Agawam Triptych, 1950
Oil on canvas
a. Left: *First Quarter*
   50 x 40 in. (127 x 101.6 cm.)
   Lent by the artist
b. Center: *Oblique of Agawam*
   50 x 40 in. (127 x 101.6 cm.)
   Marian Willard, New York
c. Right: *Third Quarter*
   50 x 40 in. (127 x 101.6 cm.)
   Mr. and Mrs. Moses Lasky, San Francisco

2.
Peyote Candle, 1951
Oil on canvas
50 x 30 in. (127 x 76.2 cm.)
Luchita Hurtado, Santa Monica, California

3.
Space Scribe (Tactile Ecstatic), 1976
(In the style of the artist's sculptures, 1950-51)
Painted wood and string
100 x 76 x 8 in. (254 x 193 x 20.3 cm.)
Lent by the artist

Gordon Onslow Ford
Born 1912, Wendover, England
Lives in Inverness, California

4.
A Present for the Past, 1942
Oil on canvas
37 x 46 in. (94 x 116.8 cm.)
The Estate of Jacqueline Onslow Ford

5.
Dwellers in the Clear, 1945
Oil on canvas
40 x 50½ in. (101.6 x 128.3 cm.)
Lent by the artist

6.
Twig Alphabet, 1950
Casein
9 x 10½ in. (22.9 x 26.7 cm.)
Lent by the artist

7.
Out of the Woods, 1951
Casein
18½ x 24½ in. (47 x 62.2 cm.)
Lent by the artist

Wolfgang Paalen
Born 1905/1907 (?), Vienna, Austria
Died 1959, Yucatan, Mexico

8.
Face, ca. 1945
Oil on canvas
16¼ x 13 in. (41.3 x 33 cm.)
Los Angeles County Museum of Art

9.
Planetary Face, 1947
Oil on canvas
59 x 55¼ in. (149.9 x 140.3 cm.)
San Francisco Museum of Modern Art

10.
Model for a Large Monument, 1948
Wood
104½ x 18 x 15½ in. (265.4 x 45.7 x 39.4 cm.)
Isabel Paalen, Mexico City

11.
Tropical Night, 1948
Oil on canvas
58½ x 55 in. (148.6 x 139.7 cm.)
Mr. and Mrs. Robert Anthoine, New York

3.

Los Angeles Hard-Edge: The Fifties and the Seventies

LACMA organized the *Four Abstract Classicists* exhibition in 1959. Writing in his foreword to the catalog, James Elliott, then chief curator, recognized "Peter Selz of the Museum of Modern Art who was active in initiating the exhibition" and "Jules Langsner, who played a major role in its organization" and who wrote the now celebrated introduction. In it Langsner (who later organized for us the first major Man Ray retrospective in 1966) wrote that "Abstract Classicist painting is hard-edge painting. Forms are finite, flat, rimmed by a hard clean edge.... They are autonomous shapes, sufficient unto themselves as shapes... presented in uniform flat color running border to border.... Color and shape are one and the same entity.... It is helpful to unite the two elements in a single word—colorform." The exhibition traveled to the San Francisco Museum of Art and then, in an altered version, to the Institute of Contemporary Art, London, and Queens College, Belfast.

In London, Lawrence Alloway at the ICA seized the phrase "hard-edge," retitled the show *West Coast Hard-Edge,* and argued that the quality of the "rigorous and exacting easel pictures" from Los Angeles should "modify the smog of legend of Los Angeles" art, and the older "constant misrepresentations" of it in art criticism. Writing later, in *Art International,* Alloway interestingly noted that in these paintings there "is an acceptance of painting as a visual object which hits the spectator's eye in ways that encourage a kind of 'illusion.' This separates such work from geometric forms of abstract art, which it sometimes appears to resemble. Decisively unlike earlier abstract art is the rejection of all separated forms (the clear fragments of Euclid which Suprematist and De Stijl painters liked) and the use of forms which involve the whole picture area, from edge to edge."

We have re-created the main look of the shows as seen in Los Angeles and London, working closely with Karl Benjamin in Claremont, Lorser Feitelson in Los Angeles, and Frederick Hammersley in Albuquerque. Nicholas Wilder in Los Angeles, the late John McLaughlin's representative, was also completely cooperative. With their help we also selected recent paintings by each artist. Working with them was continually a pleasure.

Three scholars were commissioned to write about the artists, with particular reference to their work then and now. **Susan C. Larsen,** contributing an essay on John McLaughlin, is assistant professor, University of Southern California, and specializes in American abstract art of the thirties. **Diane DeGasis Moran,** who here writes on Lorser Feitelson, teaches art history at Western Kentucky University, Bowling Green, Kentucky. **Merle Schipper,** providing us with the Karl Benjamin essay, teaches modern art history at UCLA Extension and has researched Jean Hélion's abstract phase. **Van Deren Coke's** article is a reprint of his introduction to Frederick Hammersley's 1975 retrospective exhibition at the Art Museum, University of New Mexico, of which he is director.

M. T.

Karl Benjamin

Merle Schipper

For Karl Benjamin the *Four Abstract Classicists* exhibition in 1959 was an occasion to announce his commitment to the abstract principles he had been exploring for ten years. He had, in fact, described his own work as "abstract classicist" earlier.[1]

As early as 1951 Benjamin was painting abstractions from still life, flower, figure, and landscape themes; already his works tended toward flat, frontal, and immaculately ordered compositions. His images were crisp and clean with sharply defined edges; descriptive outline was abandoned. A renegade from Abstract Expressionism, he forecast the multiple turnabout years later when several Los Angeles artists — Larry Bell, Craig Kauffman and Ed Moses, among others — reacted against their own earlier response to Action Painting.[2] Their defection from rapid, spontaneous gesture was embodied in the creation of a style which came to be labeled the "L. A. Look."[3] It was an emphatic echo to Benjamin's earlier stance.

Benjamin has quoted Paul Darrow, chairman of the art department at Scripps College, in reference to this phenomenon. Darrow once suggested that the reason California artists, no matter what their style, made paintings with such beautiful paint quality was that they saw only reproductions. Whether or not this is true for the others, Benjamin admits that it was so for him, remarking on Frank Stella, whose actual canvases surprised him by revealing brush marks and irregularities which escape the camera lens.[4]

More recently, Peter Plagens has commented on *Four Abstract Classicists*. In his view, it revealed "a current of sensibility in the esthetic climate of Los Angeles," adding, "Hard Edge arose out of Los Angeles' desert air, youthful cleanliness, spatial expanse, architectural tradiiton...and, most vaguely and most importantly, out of optimism...."[5]

Undoubtedly, the factors listed by Plagens were encouraging to Benjamin, but other elements had affected his sensibility before this exposure occurred. Benjamin was twenty-two when he arrived in Southern California. Born in Chicago in 1925, he grew up in an environment dominated by the regularized grids of Chicago architecture. This impact may have been subliminal but it underscored the visual order which marked his immediate surroundings.

These are not the only concerns reflected in the Benjamin home which stands today in Claremont, California. The house, designed by architect Fred McDowell, built in 1955, is a declaration of the honest use of materials such as natural wood and glass, and simple, straightforward post and beam construction. From this approach, design emerges as the external expression of the internal concept. Along with the studio at the rear, the garden is part of the whole *gestalt*. Abundant growth in the garden staves off rigidity and artificial formality, but it is marked by the presence of care and control on the part of the planner/gardener, the artist himself.

Almost completely absent in this setting, both indoors and out, is applied color. Natural — and this includes a garden corner accent of a singing yellow cockateel — and neutral tones prevail. In bold contrast to their surroundings, the paintings which hang in the studio, home, and even the garden exploit color to the fullest degree, for, in the artist's view, the domain of spectral color is the canvas. As personal and organic factors are ever-present in the environment, they characterize the paintings as well.

Benjamin sees himself as a "humanist" abstractionist. He is concerned with the communication of his own feelings and responses through the expressiveness of

1.
Karl Benjamin, Long Beach Museum, Long Beach, 1958.

2.
The Last Time I Saw Ferus, 1957-66, Newport Harbor Art Museum, Newport Beach, 1976, n.p. The artists named were members of the group exhibiting.

3.
Peter Plagens, *Sunshine Muse,* New York, 1974, 117-138

4.
This and other views and statements not otherwise cited here have been drawn from transcriptions of taped interviews between Benjamin and Robin Palanker for the UCLA Oral History Project, Los Angeles Art Community: *Group Portrait,* August 1976.

5.
Plagens, *Sunshine Muse*, 119-120.

color. Thus, the predilection to crisp and clear juxtapositions does not result in cold non-objectivity, but heightens the impact of color.

His preference for oil reinforces this position. Acrylics, which he has tried, lack the depth, richness of color, inherent liveliness, and response to the resilient canvas that he finds in oil. "It's beautiful and sensuous and has 'feel' to it," he has remarked. Patient and exacting by temperament, he finds the slower drying time more accommodating to his demands. "Each stage has a certain completeness about it and I like to live with that for awhile. Sometimes I get ideas for other paintings from these stages. They suggest directions that are often more reductive."[6]

Benjamin may prepare a color sketch or collage beforehand, which is necessary perhaps for only the first paintings in a series: the scheme is worked out, and changes and adjustments are made. What emerges is unsullied and unlabored; a single, flat, even coat of color.

That there are no visible brush marks or irregularities of thickness or edge is important in the attainment of purity and clarity. For Benjamin, the elimination of reflections which break down the color and disrupt the unity of the color field is essential. In the artist's view, this does not otherwise contribute to "feeling,"[7] which is achieved by color, his major interest.

Benjamin's style found its first impulse in Cubism. His early representational work, begun in 1947, shows this, but he was sensitive to color even then, and consequently was attracted to Gris and Feininger. Within their shared concern for atmosphere, their distinctly personal mood statements reflect very different esthetic sensibilities. The rich, heady luminosity of Gris' color-shapes contrast sharply with Feininger's evocation of otherwordly transcendence through diaphanous overlays of light. To Benjamin, the two represented the outermost reaches of the breadth of expressive content he sought to achieve in his own work. In recognizing the extremes, he mastered the gamut of feeling-quality that lay between.

By 1959, Benjamin's interest in Feininger's transparent quality had diminished, but his affinity with that artist in other respects lingered. *Yellow, Ochre, Umber,* 1959,

retains traces of architectural imagery, seen through the golden rays of the summer sunset (cat. no. 3). Jagged and oblique streaks dart about, interlocked with planes which tip, tilt, or fold. These are held stable by vertical attenuations of hues which reach the full height of the canvas. Perhaps it is a recollection of the Chicago skyline of his early years; the densely packed field suggests the bustling energy of urban rush hour, saturated with a warm and quieting light.

The zigzag shapes of both paintings hauntingly recall figures, but it is color that plays the chief role. It orders the paintings; it forms them. A third work from the early group reinforces this. *Big Magenta with Green,* 1959, (not shown in the original Los Angeles show; it appeared in *West Coast Hard-Edge* in London), is a bold step away from the all-over broken field; the large plane takes over the canvas, insistently forcing the high-keyed yellow and green fragments to the upper and right framing edges, from which they are about to float off into space (cat. no. 2). Until this canvas, color harmonies were generally restrained and gentle, juxtapositions smooth and prudent. *Big Magenta with Green's* vibrant chroma opened the way for startling contrast and eye-saturating intensity. These factors have continued to characterize much of Benjamin's work.

Since 1959 color has become increasingly dominant. To achieve this, Benjamin has tended to minimize structure, often (and, since 1964, entirely) eschewing irregular planes. The reduction to simple geometric shapes, whether as repeated units on a basic grid or a large edge-to-edge canvas divisions, has served to prevent the subverting of the color impact by overassertive forms. Moreover, as Alber's *Homage to the Square* has shown, reducing the format to measured primary shapes makes it easily repeatable. Within a series, where shape is constant, color is the variable and the conveyor of expressiveness.

Benjamin's commitment to color distinguishes his work from the geometric abstraction which emerged in Europe before World War II. He admits an emotional response to Mondrian, but not to the relational concerns of Neoplasticism. For Benjamin, mathematics is a useful tool to expedite the structuring process, but color is the primary agent for order as well as expression.

6.
Benjamin, in conversation with the author, 26 October 1976.

7.
Karl Benjamin's letter to Sidney Tillim, 17 January appears in Karl Benjamin, June Harwood, Peter Selz, "Setting the Record Straight," *The Los Angeles Institute of Contemporary Art Journal,* 5, 1975, 15.

Karl Benjamin
Bars No. 7, 1959
Oil on canvas
40 x 50 in. (101.6 x 127 cm.)
Los Angeles County Museum of Art
Gift of Mrs. Florence M. Arnold

A later 1959 work in the Los Angeles County Museum of Art's collection illustrates this. *Bars No. 7,* (see illustration) one of a series based on a modular grid and dominated by horizontal bars, is dependent on the qualitative factors of color, not its geometrical organization, for both the reading and response it elicits in the viewer. Painted in red, white, blue, and black, it maintains the zigzag excitement of the group of paintings executed before 1959. The activity is here achieved through the stepping up or down of the color bars and the shifting of planes; the deep blue and black tend to merge into a single dark and sonorous field.

Despite his inclusion in the *The Responsive Eye,* 1965, exhibition at the Museum of Modern Art, Benjamin is not an "Op" painter. Fluctuations, vibrations, after-images, and other retinal phenomena are not predetermined, nor is the artist concerned with complex color theory or systems. Nevertheless, Op Art sensations do occur and do play a part in releasing the expressive content. *No. 27, 1968,* (see illustration) in the collection of the Los Angeles County Museum of Art is a case in point. One of a group which the artist calls his "Module Series," the work was organized beginning with the smallest units, the quadrants of triangles, and ending with the entire painting of 144 squares. The viewer reverses the process, breaking the painting down from the whole to the quadrants. Optical vibration of the twelve pure hues at full chroma prevents one from reckoning the elementary system employed. Instead, one sees the painting forming and reforming through chromatic shifts as hues group and regroup. Viewing does not end here with the impact on the retina but enters into perceptual experience.

Benjamin's systems, when used, are never complicated, mechanical, or rigid. They are governed by intuition. He trusts his impulses for "rightness"; the determining factor is his own visual satisfaction.

With respect to this, another aspect of the artist's life is revelant. Benjamin teaches sixth grade in the farm labor community of Chino, California. He does not teach art but rather furnishes a creative ambiance that is present in the classroom throughout the school day. It is devoid of the inhibiting factors which frequently attend the elementary school "art lesson." His pupils reap rewards from the guidance they receive and the experience in art elicits a high-level response in return.

The process works both ways. The teacher gains spiritual feeedback (and often practical assistance, for the pupils sometimes color the shapes of his preparatory collages or sketches) from them. He has learned directness and daring and, most important, the immediate and joyful response to stimuli which children have not yet "learned" to repress.

Immediate and joyful response to stimuli is communicated through Benjamin's most recent work. Two color field paintings, part of a larger series, illustrate this in the present exhibiton: *#22, 1976* and *#25, 1976* (cat. nos. 4, 5). In the former, an orange field is fenced off at the surface by a central horizontal band of narrow, vertical green strips. Blue strips interpenetrate but diminish in size as they proceed from canvas edge to center. Turned obliquely, they appear to recede.

In *#25, 1976,* the blue field is held in check by shallow wedges of strips dropped from the upper edge, and, inversely mirrored, rise from the lower. Three different reds make up the strips which are graduated in length according to hue.

#22, 1976 is an expansive painting, with an illusionistic play between deep space and surface. *#25, 1976* complements it with compression and surface tension among the strips of the shallow wedges. Both are commanding presences of freshness and clarity; both are exhilarating and exultant expressions, even as they differ perceptually.

These are mature paintings, the rewards of many years of patient exploration. Color does not dazzle the eye; it radiates from the canvas to penetrate the environment. The color tends to tremble with vitality rather than vibrate in an Op Art manner.

The achievement marked by the recent work is removed from the labels of "hard edge" and "abstract classicist" with which Benjamin acknowledged his position as an abstract painter in the late 1950s. Since *Big Magenta with Green,* his engagement with color has come to the fore; he has consistently pursued his intention. The paintings of 1976 fulfill his goal of chromatic saturation which conveys expressive power and personal style.

Karl Benjamin
No. 27, 1968
Oil on canvas
79 x 79 in. (200.7 x 200.7 cm.)
Los Angeles County Museum of Art
Gift of the artist
Photo courtesy of the Jefferson
Gallery,
Los Angeles

3.
Karl Benjamin
Yellow, Ochre, Umber, 1959

1.
Karl Benjamin
Blue, Black, Grey, White, 1958

2.
Karl Benjamin
Big Magenta with Green, 1959

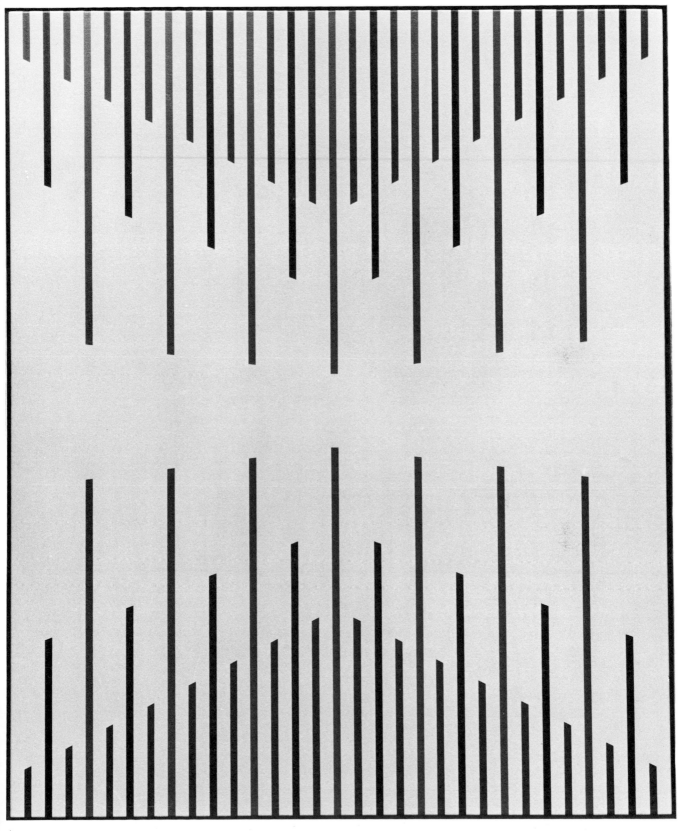

4.
Karl Benjamin
#22, 1976

Lorser Feitelson

Diane DeGasis Moran

Through a career in which classicism has been variously praised and vilified, Lorser Feitelson has been a constant and bold champion of its principles.[1] From youthful student of the Old Masters to mature prophet of Hard-Edge, he has independently explored its possibilities, reviving traditional forms of its aesthetic and discovering new and vital means of classic expression which expand its boundaries.

As a young man growing up in New York, Feitelson regularly visited the Metropolitan Museum, concentrating on the Italian Renaissance and Mannerist artists. Feitelson's early training in Renaissance and Mannerist theory is the foundation upon which his own art is built.

The Armory Show of 1913 had its impact on Feitelson; he visited it frequently. What he had seen before only on the pages of art journals was now set before him in stunning display. Recognizing the exciting possibilities which lay ahead in modern art, he resolved to make painting his life's work. In the shifting contours of Cézanne's work he saw significant implications for perceptual kinetics. He was attracted to the sense of movement in Duchamp's work he saw at the Armory Show. Feitelson's interest in perceptual kinetics continued until 1920 when it was integrated within the context of his neo-classical works and became a central concern in his later works — paintings of astonishing simplicity and elegance. The Armory Show gave Feitelson the opportunity to experience the paintings of Gauguin and Matisse, whose rhythmic and sensual contours strongly appealed to him. Throughout Feitelson's career there has been a consistent desire to synthesize the geometric and the curvilinear. Many of the polarities that George Rowley discovered in Oriental painting — expansion and contraction, void and weight, delicacy and power, and improvisation and preparation[2] — are among those that constitute Feitelson's content and form.

In the years following the Armory Show, Feitelson had contact with the leaders of American avant-garde art — Henri, Sloan, Pach, Davies, Pascin, Lachaise, and others. It did not alter his essentially isolated pursuits; the pattern which had been tentatively formed during his youth, that of independent study and experiment, became firmly set during these years. Entirely self-sufficient and sustained by art itself, Feitelson has not felt the need to join a movement, nor has he depended upon dialogue with his contemporaries. To say that he is inner-directed, which one must, implies that he is art-directed; for art has always been totally integrated within his life. Yet his own work has never been a simple reaction to another movement nor mere extension of mode. He has conceived his own aesthetic problems and found their solutions independently.

In a series of figure paintings of 1919-20, Feitelson investigated the possibilities for kinetics in the Mannerist element of *figura serpentinata*.[3] This spiraling form reached its most inspired development in the sculpture of Giovanni da Bologna, which Feitelson had admired as a youth. Feitelson's paintings and drawings included these spiral forms along with other Mannerist devices such as tension, pressure, and tangency, in combination with certain Futurist techniques. In the fifties and sixties he was to deal with identical concerns in purely abstract forms.

In 1919, on the first of several extended trips he would make to Paris during the following decade, Feitelson found himself in the midst of a neo-classical revival. The city was exhausted; in the words of Paul Valéry, "We civilizations know that we are mortal." People longed to reconstruct the war-torn world, yet political uncertainty made it impossible. Artists were sated with and distrustful of the polemical spirit of the radical pre-War movements, each of which had been championed as the true path toward artistic progress. It

1.
Information for this article is based on conversations with the artist since 1974 and on related research for a doctoral dissertation now in progress at the University of Virginia. This project was begun under the guidance of the late William C. Seitz, to whose memory this is dedicated with profound respect and gratitude.

2.
George Rowley, *Principles of Chinese Painting*, Princeton, 1947.

3.
G. P. Lomazzo, in his *Trattato* of 1584, described this form as being "...like the twisting of a live snake in motion, which is also the form of a waving flame." See John Shearman, *Mannerism: Style and Civilization*, Baltimore, 1967, 81.

seemed to many young artists that the road to artistic salvation must parallel that of social and political reclamation, by means of the restoration of order, structure, and traditional "deathless" values. The French poet-critic Blaise Cendrars, discussing the post-War decline of Cubism, wrote, "The 'home from the Front' generation has its mind aroused by other problems, and its researches point in a new direction. First of all it feels very much its own master. It wants to construct.... The young have a sense of reality. They abhor a vacuum; they abhor destruction. They want to construct...."[4] Cries of back to Poussin! back to Ingres! back to Cézanne! rang through Paris. Picasso, Matisse, and Derain, the triumvirate of the School of Paris, looked in that direction as well.

Feitelson's neo-classical paintings were multi-directional works which reflected a wide range of influences: Derain's bridging of nature and abstraction by means of angular, primitive forms as well as Matisse's development of the autonomous lyrical and sensual line; ultimately Feitelson's work was a synthesis of the two. The possibility for the harmonious coexistence of such dissimilar elements has continued to intrigue Feitelson; and it is the premise upon which a major body of his mature work is based. His later neo-classical pictures, the *Peasant* series, from the late twenties and early thirties, were explorations within High Renaissance compositions of the dynamics of directional suggestion. Discoveries in this area led directly to the principles upon which he and the California artist Helen Lundeberg founded the movement which they called Subjective Classicism or post-Surrealism, one of the few authentic American responses to Surrealism.

Feitelson's earliest post-Surrealist imagery, rich with ambiguous symbolism, was predominantly, though not entirely, representational. Over the next few years, however, abstract forms of a highly subjective nature assumed increasing significance within those compositions. By 1944 he had abandoned all vestiges of representation to concentrate exclusively on these mysterious forms, which he called post-Surrealist Configurations. It is significant that during 1942 and 1943, concurrent with the transitional post-Surrealist works, he painted a series of unabashedly romantic pictures — allegorical confessions which were introspective and subjective in nature. Characterized by rich tenebrous color, and high evocative figure compositions, these works explored the mysterious and magical realms of human sexuality and love.

Within this frame of reference were born the important "Magical Forms," those remarkable, extra-worldly, aggressively evocative, concrete materializations of conceptual forms. Simultaneously metallic and fleshily organic, but always hard-edged, they are monumental presences which teeter precariously and span dimensions of multi-horizoned space.

By 1948 Feitelson had coalesced his interest in the multiple ambiguities of the "Magical Forms" in a singular concern with spatial ambiguity. The resulting series, which, until one apprehends fully its developmental consistency with earlier work, seems to be a complete and abrupt re-direction, culminated in the paintings exhibited in the *Four Abstract Classicists* show and led in turn to the dynamic line paintings of the sixties and seventies.

Feitelson has been a force in California modernism since his arrival in Los Angeles in 1927. As painter, teacher, lecturer, and gallery director, he has tirelessly promoted advanced art.

During the early thirties, Feitelson provided crucial encouragement to adventurous young painters in the Los Angeles area. His own mobility in New York and Paris art circles during the teens and twenties had provided him with the professional sophistication which appealed to the younger generation of painters, and he opened their eyes to a wide range of art.

Philip Guston recalls Feitelson as an important mentor during his formative years in Los Angeles. Dore Ashton, quoting Guston in her recent monograph, wrote, "For Guston, Feitelson 'opened up the vistas of the Renaissance masters when I was ready for them.'"[5] Guston remembers clearly the occasion on which Feitelson took him and a few other enthusiastic young artists to see the important modern art collection of Louise and Walter Arensberg in their house in Hollywood. It is not inconceivable that this event paralleled Feitelson's own youthful experience at the Armory Show. It was in Feitelson's studio that Guston and his friends had access to a number of international art journals, otherwise difficult to obtain in the area.

4.
Blaise Cendrars, "Pourquoi le 'Cube' s'effrite?" *La rosé rouge,* Paris, 15 May 1919, 33-35.

5.
Dore Ashton, *Yes, But...A Critical Study of Philip Guston,* New York, 1976, 20.

6.
In conversation with the author, 2 February 1976, Chicago.

Jackson Pollock, though never Feitelson's student was associated with this younger group before he left Los Angeles for New York in 1930. Pollock author Francis V. O'Connor has suggested that the attitude which spawned Abstract Expressionism was attributable in part to Feitelson's early role in the Los Angeles art scene. He succinctly stated, "Feitelson *was* modern art in Los Angeles in the thirties."[6]

Walter Hopps has acknowledged the importance of Feitelson's role during the thirties and forties as "standard bearer for the vanguard in Southern California." He views Feitelson as a kind of art counterpart of those western writers whom Edmund Wilson, in his chronicles of the twenties and thirties, referred to as "the Boys in the Back Room," — creative artists aware of and responsive to their distance from cultural centers of the world. Hopps recalls Feitelson as a "peripatetic gallery-goer" during those years and as "an older and distinguished artist who had made it," but who nonetheless took great interest in the younger generation of Los Angeles artists. Attracted to certain examples of Craig Kauffman's work, for instance, Feitelson spoke highly of it to dealer Felix Landau. In turn, commented Hopps, Kauffman was "absolutely turned on" by Feitelson's work.[7]

The late art historian William C. Seitz was aware not only of Feitelson's role in the development of California art but also of the significance of his achievements in the field of perceptual movement and space based on minimal means. Of Feitelson's *Hard-Edge Line Painting*, 1964, which Seitz included in his 1965 show, *The Responsive Eye*, at the Museum of Modern Art, he said, "It is astonishing what those lines do spatially... [they] live in that space.... Feitelson does so much with so little in terms of space."[8]

(Large) Magical Space Forms, 1951

The series of "Magical Space Forms" were so named by Feitelson because of the tendency of shapes within the pictures to vacillate between space and form. The earliest experiments with this mysterious perceptual phenomenon of alternating positive and negative space were carried on by Feitelson in 1948, contemporary with the further development of the abstract Magical Forms. This is one of the earliest in the series which Feitelson describes as the most arcane. Feitelson

conceived of the light sulphur-yellow areas as the frontal planes of monumental three-dimensional forms which project into the picture space against areas of brilliant sky blue above the umber earth. In studies for the painting these yellow forms stopped short of the frame on the left and at the top; they were objects against a field, and their ambiguity as space and form was somewhat limited. By extending them to the limits of the frame, Feitelson increased their mutability and their mystery. In the painting the imposing diagonals relate to each other and to the corners of the container like precisely engineered architecture. Despite the absence of verticals and horizontals, a classic sense of stability prevails. Blazing colors of carefully controlled intensity and value activate forms which assert themselves on the picture surface.

Magical Space Forms, 1951

Feitelson continues his explorations of reversible "colorforms" in continuous flux and reveals further interest in wresting subjective experience from purely abstract imagery. He intended this as a metaphor of the prevailing mood of tension and unrest which characterized the Cold War period. Describing these forms as "mean and ominous," they were to suggest boulders balanced precariously. This work and the closely related *Geomorphic Metaphor*, 1950-51, in the collection of the Los Angeles County Museum of Art, are two of several paintings inspired by contemporary events. Recalls Feitelson, "The atmosphere that made Kafka was still present and inescapable."

Restricted in palette to black and white, this was Feitelson's first use of primed canvas. The pristine surface is perceived as unfilled and unlimited space — a void. Although the notion of the void was central to Ch'an and Zen painting, functioning actively as a creative force, it has been unfamiliar to Western art. An admirer of Oriental art for many years, Feitelson was well aware of this phenomenon, employing it here and in the revolutionary "Dichotomic Organizations" of the mid and late fifties.

Underlying its kinesthetic thrusts and counterthrusts, its tangents and pressures, its precarious balance, and its perceptual flux is a composition of unassailable structure. Formal clarity and inner structure control subjective content.

7.
In conversation with the author, 3 May 1976, Charlottesville, Virginia.
8.
In conversation with the author, 2 March 1976, Charlottesville, Virginia.

6.
Lorser Feitelson
(Large) Magical Space Forms, 1951

7.
Lorser Feitelson
Magical Space Forms, 1951

Dichotomic Organization, 1959

A series of paintings which Feitelson called
"Dichotomic Organizations," begun in the mid-1950s,
were the direct result of explorations of Mannerist
theories. They represent his efforts to create a new set
of abstract principles which, in their deliberate discord,
unstable balance, and mood of disquiet and tension
were the very antithesis of classical harmony. By
traditional standards a picture had to be unified; thus
Feitelson's first act was to divide the picture into two
equal parts. The second was to leave one of those parts
devoid of form. These were startling, courageous steps.
The human psyche naturally seeks the security of a
dominant, central image. Moreover, to the Western eye
a void is profoundly disturbing; even Feitelson himself
was not certain he could "leave it alone." This work is
painted in light coral-red, sky blue, and black. Its
palette, however, is not the real subject of the painting;
rather, it is the compositional structure and the
paradoxical subjective effects. As Langsner commented,
"Such paintings produce a disquieting 'togetherness'
and a unity where, optically speaking, a unity should
not exist."[9] The solution to this puzzle lies in the
dynamics of the void, in its innate power to
counterbalance opposing forces. It is not surprising
that Feitelson should intuit this phenomenon of
Oriental aesthetics after a lifetime of concern with
structural dynamics.

Untitled, 1971

The minimal character and graceful quality belie the
rigorous discipline of the formal problems — a concern
for the relationship of the container to the contained.
Literally extending his line over the edge of the canvas,
Feitelson intended it to be perceived as one which
continued into infinity, yet paradoxically was
"complete" within the picture. It had to be, in his
words, "a fragment total," entirely self-sufficient as an
aesthetic statement. A constant in this series is the
"lineform" which enters from below. The individual
quality of the line is crucial. Feitelson was especially
intrigued with the hermaphroditic possibilities of line,
which he admired in Oriental art. It is in these line
paintings, that Feitelson's lifetime interest in
perceptual kinetics within structured form attains its
most complete expression. Within the lines, refined,
distilled, and purified, are the aesthetic impulses of
Feitelson's entire career.

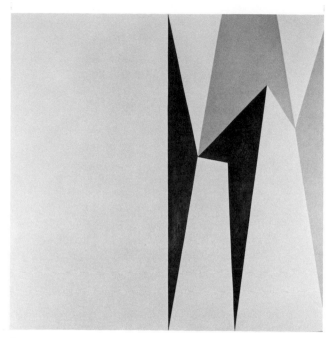

8.
Lorser Feitelson
Dichotomic Organization, 1959

9.
Jules, Langsner, "Permanence and Change in the Art of
Lorser Feitelson," *Art International,* 25 September 1963, 76.

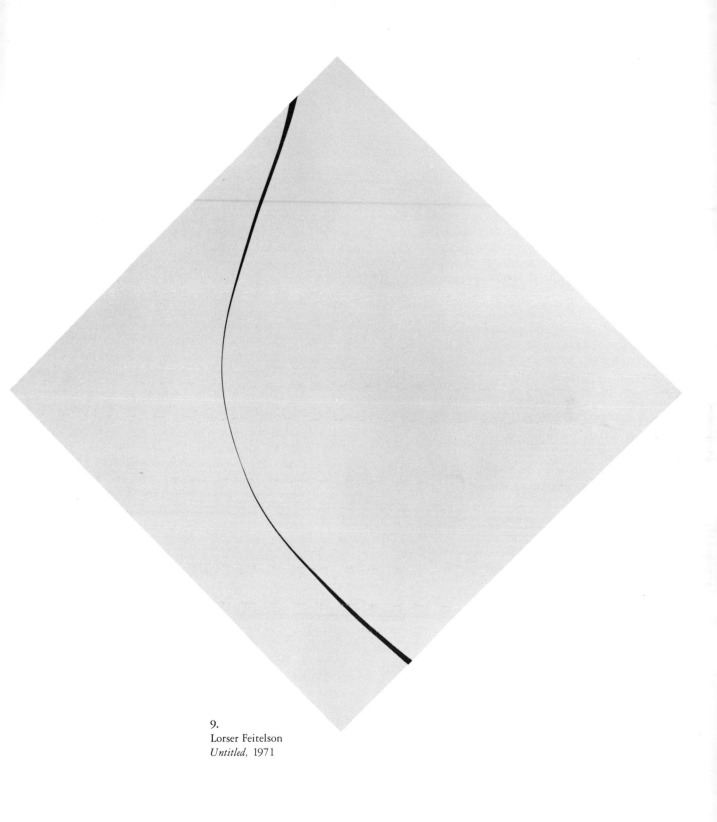

9.
Lorser Feitelson
Untitled, 1971

Frederick Hammersley[1]

Van Deren Coke

Frederick Hammersley, a Westerner by birth, training and preference, is one of America's classic hard edge painters. He attended Chouinard and Jepson art schools in Los Angeles and later taught at both of these prominent schools as well as at Pomona College for nine years before joining the faculty of the University of New Mexico in 1968. In 1971 he decided to give up teaching, remain in Albuquerque, and devote all of his time and energies to painting.

His work has been exhibited often in the West in a number of major one-man shows: Pasadena Art Museum (1961), California Palace of the Legion of Honor, San Francisco (1962), La Jolla Art Museum (1963), Santa Barbara Museum of Art (1965), and the Art Museum, University of New Mexico, Albuquerque (1969). At the same time his paintings and drawings were included in important invitational exhibitions in other parts of this country and in Europe: *Geometric Abstraction in America,* Whitney Museum of American Art, New York City (1962), *The Responsive Eye,* Museum of Modern Art, New York City (1965), *Computer Drawings,* Krannert Museum of Art, University of Illinois, Champaign (1968), the traveling exhibition, [Four] *Abstract Classicists,* shown at the Institute of Contemporary Art, London, England; Queen's University, Belfast, Ireland; San Francisco Museum of Art and Los Angeles County Museum of Art (1959-60), *Computer Drawings,* Simon Frazer University, Vancouver, Canada, and Institute of Contemporary Art (1969-70).

In 1973 Hammersley was awarded a John Simon Guggenheim Memorial Fellowship and in 1975 he received a National Endowment for the Arts grant.

During the period 1946-49 Hammersley studied one year at Chouinard Art School and two years at Jepson Art School after which he found his work at a

standstill. While at Jepson he did some teaching with Rico Lebrun. The experience of talking to students caused him to think of various ways to break out of the somewhat academic training he himself had undergone. One path was suggested to him by a design experiment he had undertaken in which he used a structure of 16 squares within a square working with a color series. This problem was absorbing enough to engage his attention for a year and a half using variations of black and white squares printed as lithographs. One of the last still life compositions he did while at Jepson was in four colors — red, yellow, black and white. From this an abstraction was drawn, then 14 color variations were tried using the same four colors.

After leaving school he made abstractions of still lifes and self portraits searching for something that felt right. The first hard edge painting came about by accident in 1950. He had divided a small canvas into 16 rectangles on which he intended to paint a self portrait. As he looked at these rectangles he could see in his mind's eye a blue in one shape. There followed a debate with himself. He asked, should I risk wasting a canvas by painting that blue, or should I do a portrait? He painted in the blue. Directly after he could see an ochre would go in another place. Then each shape came with its color until the canvas was complete. He was so astonished and pleased that he burst out laughing. There was also in this experience an awareness of *building* a painting.

To conserve material and because he was somewhat fearful of this new approach he started working on small sheets of paper with colored pencils. He would look at a blank page and see a shape. That shape would produce another and so on. After many of these colored pencil "paintings" he tried working on canvas with oil paint. The fact that these shapes grew or were built up

1.
This first appeared in *Frederick Hammersley, A Retrospective Exhibition,* University of New Mexico, Art Museum, 1975. The author has kindly granted us permission to reprint the essay.

of themselves made it seem appropriate to use a building tool to apply paint. He chose a trowel-shaped palette knife for this purpose. To eliminate time between the impulse and application, color was used, unmixed, directly from the tube. In time his palette consisted of 75 different tubes of color. Many panels and canvases were prepared. He recalls, "When I'd be attracted to one I'd look at it until I'd know what color it would be." He would then paint that canvas its color. Due to the slow drying of the oil paint he would have from 10 to 14 canvases in process at one time. He became aware of a phenomenon new to him. Since he did not paint until he could "see" that shape, nothing was ever changed once painted. He also always knew when the last shape was put in and the painting finished.

The canvases he worked on during this period were small to medium size, the longest side being thirty-nine inches. The second stage of his development occurred as the canvases became larger — up to fifty inches. When some shapes were painted and no impulse would come he would try to prod the process by drawing shapes in charcoal. The ones that did not work he would erase, and paint the ones that fit to his satisfaction. At times everything would come to a halt. He would return to drawing by himself or with friends.

In the third and current stage he began the creative process by drawing an idea in a notebook. Perhaps because of this the newer paintings have evolved into fewer shapes in contrast to the many shapes of the earlier works.

Often an idea comes full blown. He draws its structure and then follows with colors. At other times a portion of an idea comes. He draws that, then attempts to bring the rest of it together by more drawing.

It now seems that the fewer the shapes the longer it takes for him to get an idea.

After an idea is established in his notebook he lets it age for a few weeks to a year before committing it to canvas. He has said recently, "I know when I have a good one but I let it sit awhile to test it." When he finally sets down his forms they are unequivocally themselves and without any reference to volume, weight or an allusion to recession in depth.

Hammersley has found fulfillment in the adventure that ends with each new picture. His paintings now range from lyrical quivering shapes and colors to simple, forthright black and white combinations. They all are so resolutely conceived and executed that we tend to overlook an unusual and consistent characteristic that many of them have. This is a sense of joviality or spirit of optimism. We notice it first in his titles. They are each chosen carefully after Hammersley sits down and looks at each picture afresh. A waggishness that is nicely autobiographical frequently comes into play at this point. Primarily, however, Hammersley is interested in the refinement of psychic impulses that in his case seem to come in geometric packages ready to be unfolded onto canvas. All is up front for us to see. The clarity of his formal statements speaks eloquently of the firm control he has over his hand as well as his intellect. There is no arbitrariness, no underlying structure pattern. He is a painter in the traditional sense of the word. No sprayed color or masking tape for him. Each passage is painted thereby taking advantage of the subtle surface modulation assumed by the pigment and the ever so slight alterations to the edges of his forms that cause them to vibrate against one another. While he does not paint pictures of things, in no sense does he ignore the world about him or for that matter the inner world of intuition. The combinations of color in flowers fascinate him as do the designs of Navajo rugs. When he feels he is in a slump and a new direction is needed he turns to his camera and makes macrophotographs of blossoms or does hundreds of quick sketches of heads that are drawn out of his subconscious — thus releasing the mind from the rigidity it had taken when following a restricted course he had set.

The hardest thing to do when painting in as unadorned a style as Hammersley's is to maintain a sense of surprise and avoid the danger of being merely decorative. This he does with a high degree of consistency. What happens is that he is completely honest in his choice of forms and colors and the seemingly clinical quality of the vocabulary he uses never puts us off or strains our enjoyment of what he has evolved. To say this in another way — the tone, style and spirit of the man is manifest in the work he does.

12.
Frederick Hammersley
Like unlike, 1959

14.
Frederick Hammersley
Red & alizarin green, 1958

11.
Frederick Hammersley
Red & alizarin green, 1958

15.
Frederick Hammersley
Yes and know, 1975.

John McLaughlin

Susan C. Larsen

John McLaughlin's participation in the 1959 exhibition *Four Abstract Classicists* at the Los Angeles County Museum is one of the most interesting anomalies of contemporary art. Nothing could be further from his intent and the character and structure of his work. McLaughlin's painting is profoundly anti-classical. He creates disequilibrium and virtually subliminal, visual and psychological motion out of stasis and symmetry. McLaughlin's clearly articulated forms, plain edges, and straightforward, even pedestrian, surfaces can create impenetrable walls. He does not charm us with vibrating, broken passages of paint or tighten the skin of his canvas so that it is shining, taut, with razor-sharp edges. He is often engagingly awkward, seemingly incapable of the noble harmonies of Neoplasticism — a painter who began his serious work late in life, a present-day abstract primitive, transgressor of the rules, resident of Japan and California, unconventional, out-of-the-mainstream. Working within a formal vocabulary which has become synonymous with the expansive harmonies of Newman, the brooding colorism of Rothko, the dynamic equilibrium of Mondrian, McLaughlin seeks to disturb and beguile, to entrap us in a visual experience which exhausts our perception and confounds our ability to find a stable, harmonic solution.

McLaughlin's work rejects the assumption that equilibrium and wholeness are positive goals. McLaughlin has often been compared to Mondrian, for the same reason that the work of McLaughlin's other American contemporaries, Diller, Bolotowsky, Leon Polk Smith, Reinhardt, Newman, and Kelly has been related to the pictorial syntax of Neoplasticism. Within this context, McLaughlin is another of the hard-edge and Neoplastic artists who found a personal vocabulary out of an intensive investigation of European abstract movements and the impetus of their pictorial vision. In McLaughlin's work, however, there is a specific instance in which the comparison with Mondrian is particularly useful. Mondrian's last work, created between 1938 and 1942, for example, *New York I* and *New York II, Broadway Boogie-Woogie,* and *Victory Boogie-Woogie* also rejected the goals of equilibrium and a wholeness created out of the resolution of opposing tensions. These canvases involve incessant optical scanning, the eye darting through and around a web of related forms, responding to correspondences of color, shape, scale, and perceived relationships which are only briefly retained because of their complexity and the insistent demands of other, equally assertive stimuli.

Mondrian achieved this incessant optical movement by quickening the intervals between his forms, reducing their scale, complicating internal color relationships and increasing the density of his compositions. McLaughlin came to a similar state by reducing the number of his forms, enlarging them, paring down, and clarifying the tense interplay of a few major elements. McLaughlin exhibited *#9, 1959,* (see illustration) in the Los Angeles County Museum's *Four Abstract Classicists.* Divided into three equal vertical segments, the center panel is broken into two unequal, highly contrasting parts, which arrest the eye, then send it from left to right in an effort to resolve the paradox of overall symmetry and internal symmetry. As in Mondrian's late work, the paradox is impossible to resolve; it remains before the viewer, clearly stated and impenetrable.

All of this is highly aberrant behavior for an artist working within a hard-edge format during the late fifties and early sixties. McLaughlin was sixty-one in 1959, the year of *Four Abstract Classicists.* He had spent time in the Far East, living in Japan during the late 1930s and serving in China and Burma during World

John McLaughlin
#9, 1959
Oil on canvas
60 x 38 in. (152.4 x 96.5 cm.)
Exhibited in LACMA's *Four Abstract Classicists,* 16 September-18 October, 1959. Present location unknown.

War II, from 1941 to 1945. During the late 1940s when McLaughlin settled in California, his work was quietly competent and informed, but owed a heavy debt to biomorphic Cubism, Constructivism, and Neoplasticism, styles which had long been explored in New York painting of the late 1930s. In the 1950s McLaughlin began to restrict himself to clearly defined rectangles, circles, and squares, coming to a severe, hard-edge format with a highly personal syntax by 1959. As interesting as McLaughlin's early work may be, it was during the twenty-year period between the late fifties and his death in 1976 that he created his most personal and significant canvases. At the time of *Four Abstract Classicists* McLaughlin's work appeared to have a good deal in common with contemporary developments in New York. There were even more significant differences, however, which became apparent as the superficial similarities of hard edges, evenly painted colored surfaces, and clearly defined forms gave way to considerations of image, format, expression, optical movement, symmetry, asymmetry, and the canvas as object.

With Stella, Kelly, and Diller, McLaughlin makes us aware of the shape and proportion of his canvases. Individual internal elements refer to and define themselves by their relationship to the boundaries of the surface. We focus upon the center, but we are directed outward, laterally, and the limitations of the canvas define all internal proportions. In Kelly's work, edge defines shape and the canvas becomes object-image. Stella erases internal tensions by the creation of unity out of corresponding parts. Diller releases the internal tension of his compositions with a Neoplastic device, the limitless edge — forms which are open at one end and, by implication, extend beyond the canvas. In Diller's *First Theme: Number 10,* 1963, (see illustration) present boundaries are only a framework for this particular set of relationships; the internal elements by their extension imply an infinity of space. Diller's vertical forms are almost gestural in this context.

McLaughlin, however, denies the object-image by pulling his internal forms away from the edges of the canvas. By doing this he creates highly charged figure-ground relationships and divides the surface into a sub-system of proportions which redefine the primary forms through the creation of a new context. McLaughlin is not afraid of the figure-ground

relationship; he revels in it and plays with it much as the Cubists handled figure-ground exuberantly but with respect for its visual primacy.

During the early sixties McLaughlin created a number of compositions in which rectangular elements were placed in a symmetrical configuration but not necessarily at absolutely identical intervals across a contrasting ground. These internal rectangles are often bisected by a slender line or divided into equal parts by contrasting colors. They float upon the surface of the canvas, setting up figure-ground relationships and defining a complex proportional system. Within these internal rectangles contrasting colors vibrate, emitting an insistent signal which refuses to settle into the surface of the canvas.

How can anything so evidently symmetrical, so firmly placed and regular in its intervals create such visual instability, questioning the standard analogues of symmetry and stasis? In these compositions, McLaughlin upsets the potentially static elements of his composition by doubling them. Rectangles, evenly placed and bisected, cause the eye to travel continuously across the canvas, left to right and back again, seeking a point of resolution, hoping to pull the composition together. No such point of resolution is offered. McLaughlin presents a riddle without an answer.

McLaughlin's abstract Mannerism, visually unstable, in constant motion, drawing its power from its subtle departures from apparent clarity and symmetry, is a typical anti-classical attitude. It might be compared to the spatial disjunctiveness of the Italian Mannerists, the structured paradoxes of Cubism, and even the psycho-visual motion of optical art of the 1960s. This is in marked contrast to the reductivist tendencies of other hard-edge painters working within a severe geometric format. A number of McLaughlin's paintings of the late 1960s and 1970s are composed of vertically placed rectangles which define and divide the horizontal plane. This group bears an initial resemblance to the work of Newman. Some of McLaughlin's sharp verticals appear to function as Newman's "zips," but, once again, McLaughlin brings his vertical elements in toward the center, pulling them ever-so-slightly away from the edges of the canvas. McLaughlin's scale is also smaller—some of the canvases are five feet in their larger dimension — but they are very definitely

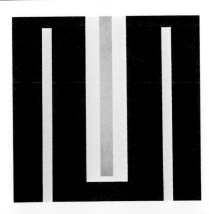

Burgoyne Diller
First Theme: Number 10, 1963
Oil on canvas
72 x 72 in. (182.9 x 182.9 cm.)
Whitney Museum of American Art,
New York
Gift of the Friends of the Whitney
Museum of American Art

easel paintings whose focus is central and whose individual elements are self-assertive, even while related to the overall system of proportions and to the edge of the canvas.

Much has been said about McLaughlin's love of Oriental aesthetics, specifically, the juxtaposition of object and void in Japanese painting of the Ashikaga Period as in the painting of Sesshu which, in turn, grew out of the work of Hsia Kuei and Ma Yuan, Chinese painters of the Southern Sung Dynasty. Ma Yuan, or "one-corner Ma" as he was called, loved to silhouette natural forms against a virtually empty background suggestive of space, mist, light, and infinity. McLaughlin's admiration of this aesthetic and pictorial concept has been well-documented; he expressed this interest in conversations and in his writing. It is another instance of his fascination with the figure-ground relationship which painters, East and West, have known is a visual and metaphysical concept basic to concepts of manifestation and dissolution, being and non-being, forever tied to the mysteries of existence.

Two of McLaughlin's Western contemporaries, Newman and Reinhardt, have also dealt with this concept within a hard-edge geometric format. Their methods are very different from McLaughlin's and brief discussion of all three may help to more closely define the nature of McLaughlin's aesthetic. Newman seeks to overwhelm and envelop; his surfaces are vibrant, with highly saturated radiant layers of pigment. His scale erases the boundaries between canvas and observer; his divisions of the surface are massive, gestural, architectural in their power. Newman's harmonic ratios create an underlying stability which is felt and recognized even as one is physically aware of the uneven divisions of his surfaces. Newman's desire to create a transcendent unity out of unequal component parts is directly expressed; one becomes attuned to the expressive power of the canvas, yielding to one's subliminal awareness of an internal order. All sense of dilemma and struggle vanish; the canvas is felt as well as seen, a blending of sensuality and the logic of vision. Newman constructs a strong harmonic chord; it convinces by the affective power of its physical presence. It is a direct confrontation; the viewer is drawn into the work, his self-awareness dissipates, he is lost in the psycho-visual experience of the work of art.

McLaughlin, on the contrary, presents an evident physical symmetry. His surfaces are evenly divided or their ratios are quickly discoverable. He pulls us toward the center, focusing our attention on some point of tension or some problem incapable of visual solution. Two long rectangles confront each other, divided by a center line which is also part of the background plane. A central rectangle hovers in space upon a contrasting background; a tense figure-ground relationship is achieved by pulling them away from two edges of the canvas. In composition after composition McLaughlin causes us to concentrate on some point of tension or puts us in a visually unstable situation. It is like fixing our attention upon the point of a pin, bringing the mind downward in an ever-descending spiral until all other stimuli vanish and the mind is caught, held and completely focused. If, in this process, McLaughlin enables us to approach a state of emptiness like the one described by the Japanese painter, it is not the oceanic feeling of Newman, an all-encompassing wholeness of all and nothing, but an intently focused, very physical and specific state of awareness.

The mental state induced by McLaughlin's plain, even awkward compositions is remarkable, like that said to be induced by the contemplation of a Zen *koan,* a riddle which is plain on the surface, composed of known elements, but poses relationships which defy logic and the mind's habit of closure. The veneer of plainness is another Zen attribute. A Zen *koan* appears as a simple homily. Nothing specifically metaphysical is suggested—the jewel poses as a rock. Zen paintings deal with everyday tasks; they use fruits and vegetables to diagram the universe, involve decay and unusual physical types, and they are often reckless to the point of chaos, an aesthetic of the irregular and the unlovely.

The apparent akwardness, the simplicity of many of McLaughlin's compositions also present this veneer of plainness. These qualities are underscored by his unpretentious surface. McLaughlin's edges are hand-painted, imperfect but clean in their articulation of forms. An artist who consciously transgresses so many of the rules of composition, who bisects his canvas, who creates intentionally unbalanced structures, who puts one odd element in a carefully constructed set of intervals and lets each of these situations speak plainly and openly is at once guileless and extremely sophisticated.

This special quality of McLaughlin's, his unexpectedness, stands in contrast to the serious reductivism of Reinhardt. Each artist escapes the constraints of the natural world, having worked his way through Cubism and Neoplasticism, coming to an extremely reduced geometric format. Each tries to focus attention upon a structured composition which will hold the mind while engaging the eye in an elusive figure-ground interplay. Reinhardt's "black" paintings bring the figure-ground relationship down to an interaction of extremely close tonalities of warm and cool blacks, defining a symmetrical cross on a square format. Visually it is the reverse of McLaughlin's bright colors and highly contrasting forms, but psychologically the two artists are engaged in a similar enterprise; an attempt to steady the mind by holding and beguiling the eye.

While sharing some of the concerns and methods of other hard-edge abstract painters, McLaughlin found his own aesthetic by the early 1960s. In the last two decades of his life, his pictorial vision became clearer, his compositions even more uncompromising in their symmetry and strength. In McLaughlin's work, color does not function symbolically but as a physical entity having a sensuous presence and a psycho-physical impact upon the eye and mind. A leanness and purity characterizes his handling of color. There is little temptation to dissociate color from shape, even less temptation to read color and structure as landscape. He is much closer to Malevich than to Diebenkorn.

All this is remarkable in an artist born in 1898, a contemporary of the Abstract Expressionists, who, in fact, was a decade older than many of them. McLaughlin must have resisted many easy temptations. He certainly knew how to construct a correct Neoplastic composition. He easily could have increased the scale of his work in the early 1960s. He could have become more overtly involved with optics during the same period; McLaughlin's optical configurations are stronger and more profound than anything that brief movement was able to produce. Through all the shared concerns and subtle differences, one senses an overriding personal discipline and integrity in his

work. He built each advance upon his own achievements; one suspects it is not an instance of a man being out of touch with the mainstream but of refusing to look for direction by looking over his shoulder. Nor was McLaughlin a recluse. Several generations of artists in California, particularly painters, have observed his dignified good humor, admired his integrity, and enjoyed personal contact and conversation.

One of the principal temptations McLaughlin resisted was to become a California artist, to allow himself or those who presented his work to take the easy road of romantic regionalism. McLaughlin is neither a California artist nor a New York artist; he is neither a Neoplasticist nor a Hard-Edge Classicist; his aesthetic is both Eastern and Western. He eludes classification, a singular achievement in an era which often equates legitimacy with classifiability.

During the year since his death, McLaughlin's achievement is being examined with greater interest than ever before, in part due to recent developments in abstract painting which have much in common with his format and intentions. Several retrospective exhibitions of the mid-1970s have acquainted a larger public and, significantly, a number of younger artists with the depth and evolution of his work. One recalls the end of the nineteenth century when several significant retrospective exhibitions occurred just after the death of major painters whose importance had been apparent to their contemporaries but was just being discovered by the next generation of artists and the general public. These occasions increased the artists' sphere of influence beyond anything they had experienced during their lifetimes and revealed the depth and scope of their achievements.

An evaluation of John McLaughlin's work is as difficult as he meant it to be. The almost impenetrable veneer of plainness holds; the painting is a meeting ground of mind and eye. It is also a place for testing. With an air of dignity and reticence he offers us a riddle. Our ability to sense its depths and find an answer is a measure of McLaughlin's vision and our own.

John McLaughlin
No. 26, 1961
Oil on canvas
36 x 48 in. (91.4 x 122 cm.)
Los Angeles County Museum of Art
Gift of Joseph Mendelson

16.
John McLaughlin
#X, 1958

17.
John McLaughlin
#16, 1958-59

18.
John McLaughlin
#12, 1959

19.
John McLaughlin
#15, 1973

20.
John McLaughlin
#2, 1974

Dimensions: height x width x depth

Karl Benjamin
Born 1925, Chicago, Illinois
Lives in Claremont, California

1.
Blue, Black, Grey, White, 1958
Oil on canvas
44 x 56 in. (111.8 x 142.2 cm.)
Mrs. Dolly Bright Carter, Beverly Hills, California

2.
Big Magenta with Green, 1959
Oil on canvas
40 x 50 in. (101.6 x 127 cm.)
Lent by the artist

3.
Yellow, Ochre, Umber, 1959
Oil on canvas
62 x 42 in. (157.5 x 106.7 cm.)
Dr. Kenneth B. Bonilla, Claremont, California

4.
#22, 1976
Oil on canvas
59½ x 44½ in. (151.1 x 113 cm.)
Tortue Gallery, Santa Monica, California

5.
#25, 1976
Oil on canvas
59½ x 47½ in. (151.1 x 120.7 cm.)
Tortue Gallery, Santa Monica, California

Lorser Feitelson
Born 1898, Savannah, Georgia
Lives in Los Angeles, California

6.
(Large) Magical Space Forms, 1951
Oil and enamel on canvas
68 x 101½ in. (172.7 x 247.8 cm.)
Lent by the artist

7.
Magical Space Forms, 1951
Oil on canvas
58 x 82 in. (147.3 x 208.3 cm.)
Lent by the artist

8.
Dichotomic Organization, 1959
Oil on canvas
60 x 60 in. (152.4 x 152.4 cm.)
Lent by the artist

9.
Untitled, 1971
Acrylic on canvas
85 x 85 (215.9 x 215.9 cm.)
Lent by the artist

10.
Untitled, 1971
Acrylic on canvas
60 x 60 in. (152.4 x 152.4 cm.)
Lent by the artist

Frederick Hammersley
Born 1919, Salt Lake City
Lives in Albuquerque, New Mexico

11.
Red & alizarin green, 1958
Oil on linen
36 x 48 in. (91.4 x 121.9 cm.)
Lent by the artist

12.
Like unlike, 1959
Oil on linen
49 x 40 in. (124.5 x 101.6 cm.)
Lent by the artist

13.
Sun substance, 1959
Oil on canvas
50 x 40 in. (127 x 101.6 cm.)
Lent by the artist

14.
Four awhile, 1974
Oil on linen
45 x 45 in. (114.3 x 114.3 cm.)
Lent by the artist

15.
Yes and know, 1975
Oil on linen
45 x 45 in. (114.3 x 114.3 cm.)
Lent by the artist

John McLaughlin

Born 1898, Sharon, Massachusetts
Died 1976, Laguna Beach, California

16.
#X, 1958
Oil on canvas
48 x 36 in. (121.9 x 91.4 cm.)
Nicholas Wilder, Los Angeles

17.
#16, 1958-59
Oil on canvas
72 x 42 in. (182.9 x 106.7 cm.)
Nicholas Wilder Gallery, Los Angeles

18.
#12, 1959
Oil on canvas
52 x 36 in. (132 x 91.4 cm.)
Nicholas Wilder Gallery, Los Angeles

19.
#15, 1973
Oil and acrylic on canvas
60 x 48 in. (152.4 x 121.9 cm.)
André Emmerich Gallery, New York

20.
#2, 1974
Acrylic on canvas
48 x 60 in. (121.9 x 152.4 cm.)
André Emmerich Gallery, New York

4.

John McLaughlin Letters and Documents

The Archives of American Art, a bureau of the Smithsonian Institution, is a research center for American visual arts from colonial times to the present. Microfilm copies of primary source material are made available to scholars and students for study at five area centers (New York City, Boston, Washington, D.C., Detroit, and San Francisco) and through inter-library loan. The original documents are preserved at the Smithsonian in Washington.

This display of selections from the John McLaughlin Papers was prepared by Paul Karlstrom, director, and his staff at the Archives' West Coast Area Center, located at the M. H. de Young Memorial Museum in San Francisco. The McLaughlin Papers represent one of the most important and complete collections gathered in the Los Angeles area. The Archives actively seeks such source material in a continuing effort to provide the information necessary to a better appreciation and understanding of the art history of this region and the nation. This memorial exhibition and the catalog essay based on the McLaughlin Papers demonstrate how the Archives may be used to that very end.

Donald F. McCallum, assistant professor of art history at UCLA, is a specialist in Japanese art, having published in *Artibus Asiae* and *Oriental Art.* He has had a longtime fascination with the painting of John McLaughlin.

M. T.

19.
Photograph of McLaughlin by John
Waggaman.

The John McLaughlin Papers in the
Archives of American Art

Donald F. McCallum

Fortunately, much material from John McLaughlin's estate, now in the possession of the Archives of American Art, offers an extraordinary range of interesting and informative documents hitherto relatively unknown. Some of this material is germane in refining our picture of John McLaughlin and his art.

McLaughlin came to painting as a vocation quite late in life, after engaging in various occupations in his earlier years. For a time, he dealt in Japanese prints; material in the Archives substantiates this phase of his life. His strong interest in Japanese language and art led him to spend the years 1935-1937 in Japan. Returning to Boston, he continued selling art; several cordial letters in the Archives from Japanese print dealers date almost to the moment of America's entry into World War II. From the immediate post-War period there is extensive correspondence related to McLaughlin's efforts to sell his print collection. Most of the letters to McLaughlin are tactful rejections. One gets the impression from the letters that McLaughlin did not own many truly important works at this time. However, the correspondence between McLaughlin and the distinguished Orientalist, Laurence Sickman, yields the following:

> I am continuing with my painting and I feel, making some progress. The San Diego Museum seems more sympathetically disposed toward nonobjective painters than other institutions hereabout so I have been showing there. Later on I shall send you a few photographs of some of my crimes. [18 June 1947]

McLaughlin's activities as a dealer bracketed his years of military service. As a result of his study of the language, he was recruited by the Army as a language officer in the Intelligence branch. The Archives includes several documents related to his war service as well as photographs of him in uniform. Since McLaughlin frequently spoke at length to interviewers about his life in the Army, further study of these years might be worthwhile.

McLaughlin and his wife Florence settled in Dana Point, California, in 1946; the majority of the McLaughlin material in the Archives collection dates from then to 1976. By the late 1940s and early 1950s McLaughlin was beginning to receive a modicum of recognition. Evidence of local success is a letter of 1948 from the Fine Arts Gallery of San Diego informing him that "... your painting 'Hope Deferred' has been awarded the first prize for Oil Painting at the San Diego Art Guild Annual."[1] In late 1951 Gordon Washburn, then director of the Carnegie Institute, wrote asking him to submit three or four photos of paintings from the last five years for consideration for the Pittsburgh International of 1952. These and other letters suggest that the art community was aware of McLaughlin from a rather early stage in his career. A clear indication of his increasing stature as an artist is the correspondence leading up to his association with the Felix Landau Gallery in Los Angeles.

Perhaps the most important documents in the Collection are those which show the development of McLaughlin's ideas about art and aesthetics. There are numerous drafts for statements published in the catalog of his one-man shows. More unusual, however, is an early statement that gives a detailed account of his ideas about art. In 1951, McLaughlin outlined his views on painting in response to a letter which he had received:

> Conceptually all my work is the same. Reality to me is an aesthetic infinity never to be fully realized. Therefore, my great struggle is to find and keep that direction. With knowledge and

1.
Awarding first prize to an abstract painting produced an amusing controversy which raged in the San Diego newspapers during the spring of 1948. The Archives contains full documentation of this incident.

understanding, the goal becomes increasingly distant and the pursuit becomes increasingly urgent. I am not preoccupied with nature, but I am concerned with my relationship to nature. My paintings, such as they are, continue to change in appearance, one from another, and apart from instinctive weaknesses which constantly appear, these changes are brought about in my efforts toward refinement and clarity of purpose (although the design may at times appear complicated). [15 January 1951]

The reference to "complicated design" is important, since at the time McLaughlin had not yet fully achieved that spare, pared-down feeling that we now associate with his work. Nevertheless, the thrust of this statement appears to foretell the subsequent development of his painting. At this early stage McLaughlin already renounced any commitment to theories:

In my case, intuition is about all I have to go on — mathematics, geometry, composition, design, color relationships, etc., etc., as such, mean nothing to me whatever. Artists, I am told, use these devices sometimes to make attractive paintings. [15 January 1951]

With comments which later became standard in McLaughlin's interviews, we can see McLaughlin himself disdaining any connection with "artiness." Later he writes about those who influenced him:

I am not possessed of an artistic nature (the dread disease from which many artists suffer) nor have I that virtuosity that keeps many artists in art schools all their lives. . . . I have no theories about painting as an art or craft but I do have principles concerning aesthetics. And I paint simply because for me a plastic statement seems to be the most effective manner of communication. The laws, if any there be, are those intangibles evidenced in the formal painting of the early Chinese and Japanese, ancient Egyptian sculpture, the observations of Aristotle and Hegel, the plays of Ibsen, the novels of Joyce and Dostoevsky, the music of Bach, Barton and Shoenberg, the painting of Cézanne and Mondrian, to mention just a few. [15 January 1951]

This remarkable letter illustrates clearly McLaughlin's ideas about painting just at the time when he began to make his unique contribution. Although it is not possible in this short essay to compare these ideas with those he developed in the later 1950s and 1960s, a full understanding of McLaughlin's thoughts about painting and aesthetics will only be possible with a careful study of the documents in the Archives.

Several interesting letters in the collection of the Archives refer to the genesis of the *Four Abstract Classicists* exhibition. Since there has been some controversy concerning this exhibition, the McLaughlin papers, used in conjunction with other documents, should be of great assistance in resolving problems. Sufficient McLaughlin papers, letters, and drafts exist in the Archives (though not necessarily *all* extant material) to provide a clear picture of the evolution of this show. In a letter from Karl Benjamin dated 29 August 1957, the plan was apparently broached for the first time. McLaughlin immediately drafted a reply, dated 31 August 1957, in which he agreed to participate, and shortly thereafter they met to discuss the project. On 11 March Peter Selz wrote to McLaughlin and referred to the fact that Jules Langsner had agreed to do a catalog essay. Following this letter, there appears to be a break in the documentation. However, there is a very extensive correspondence between McLaughlin and Langsner related to the catalog essay.

Full files of documents exist in the collection of the Archives pertaining to McLaughlin's one-man shows in the 1960s and 1970s, particularly the 1968 retrospective at the Corcoran Gallery of Art in Washington, D.C. As McLaughlin became increasingly well known, the correspondence grew in volume. The later material is generally less revealing than some of the earlier documents. Nevertheless, a complete account of McLaughlin's mature years as a painter will inevitably be based on this material.

In addition to standard documents, the Archives contains McLaughlin's sketches and models for paintings. While some of the sketches may be preliminary ideas for paintings, most appear to be records of works that had been sent to dealers or museums. More interesting, however, are the models, made of construction paper, which are the penultimate versions of the finished paintings (cat. no. 17). These must be seen in the context of McLaughlin's desire to avoid any random or accidental effects in his compositions; clearly, the total conception of the painting was worked out prior to the time the artist began executing the final canvas.

It might be suggested that there is a strong analogy between McLaughlin's methods of writing and painting. Anyone who studies the papers in the Archives will be struck by the fact that he often made numerous drafts of a single, one-page statement, altering and polishing it until the final version seemed satisfactory. This sort of careful, painstaking mode of writing left nothing to chance; rather, it aimed at a lucid, crystal-clear form of discourse. Similarly, in developing the ideas for his paintings, McLaughlin worked intensely over the material during the preliminary stages until he had achieved a form that seemed adequate to him.

The few suggestions I have made in this essay concerning the possible uses of the McLaughlin papers in the Archives of American Art do not begin to exhaust the Collection's full potentialities. As suggested, the most valuable documents seem to be those related to the artist's ideas about art and aesthetics. In particular, McLaughlin's correspondence with Jules Langsner must be carefully analyzed. In preparing his catalog essay for *Four Abstract Classicists,* Langsner sent a questionnaire to each participant; McLaughlin appears to have been very careful in drafting his answers. He wrote to Langsner outlining aspects of his art which were not covered by the questionnaire. There are other statements that give complete perspective on McLaughlin's refinement of his ideas about art. The Archives also contain documents related to sales, which should be helpful in assessing the economics of McLaughlin's career. In addition, there are several letters which may provide leads in locating early works now in private collections.

In conjunction with other Archival material, as well as with published writings, the McLaughlin papers will be of great assistance in expanding our view of John McLaughlin as an artist and as an individual.

Box 95,
Dana Point, Calif

January 15, 1951

Dear Mr. Wilson:

I was pleased to get your letter and ma
I say now that it is very reassuring to find
someone, now and again, who is sympathetic
toward my work.

I think your idea of writing a critical
paper on art in Southern California a very
good one. Artists in particular would, I am
sure, welcome any honest treatment of the subject.

From your letter I can fairly assume
that you propose to crusade for better art
utilizing as a means of comparisonthe combin-
ationof your theory of spatial organization
and certain aspects of my work.

As inviting as the prospects of fame
may be I don't think that this plan would work
My own ideas of picture organization must per-
force be my own and these I employ arbitrarily
While on the subject of my own work I might
briefly give you some clues as to what I am
seeking.

Conceptually all my work is the same.
Reality to me is an aesthetic infinity never
to be fully realized. Therefore, my great
struggle is to find and keep that direction.
With knowledge and understanding, the goal becomes increasingly distant and the pursuit becomes increasingly urgent. I am not preoccupied with nature, but I am concerned with my re-
lationshipto nature. My paintings, such as
they are, continue to change in appearance, one

from another, and apart from instinctive
weaknesses which constantly appear, these
changes are brought about in my efforts toward refinement and clarity of purpose (although the design may at times appear complicated).

In my case, intuition is about all I
have to go on -- mathematics, geometry, composition, design, color relationships etc, etc
as such, mean nothing to me whatever. Artist
s, I am told, use these devices sometimes to
make attractive paintings.

I am not possessed of an artistic
nature (the dread disease from which many
artists suffer) nor have I that virtuosity
that keeps many artists in art schools all
their lives. I am not so desirous of making
paintings as good or better than another
painter as I am to submit to and record plas-
tically the crystallization of the actual
motivating influences that somehow set into
motion an overpowering urge to say something.
The indirect influences are broad and general.
The direct influences that seem to precipitate
the actare in most cases literature and music
Now and then a fleeting visual experience may
set the machinery in motion. The idea while
in the mind burns bright-- to retain it long
enough to record its essence visually is the
critical period and may take 10 minutes or
a month. Once down in a way that satisfies,
the rest is easy. Placement, color, and the
time te it takes to put it on a board and
paint it. Beyond that, so far as I am concerned, there are no rules or laws apart from
the exercise of self discipline and integrity.

I have no theories abot painting as
an art or craft but I do have principals concerning aesthetics. And I paint simply because for me a plastic statement seems to be

5.
Letter to Mr. Wilson from McLaughlin,
15 January 1951 (four pages, typed)
containing early statement of
McLaughlin's artistic position.

the most effective manner of communication. The laws, if any there be, are those intangibles evidenced in the formal painting of the early Chinese and Japanese., ancient Egyptian sculpture, the observations of Aristotle and Hegel, the plays of Ibsen, the novels of Joyce and Dostoevsky, the music of Bach, Bartok and Shoenberg, the painting of Cezanne and Mondrian, to mention just a few.

These men, in my opinion, were not so much great writers, composers and painters as they were great men who wrote, composed and painted. And in them and in other can be found extraordinary powers of perception with the strength and skill to record their findings in a manner determined by themselves alone. And from them can be gained the lesson that aesthetic expression is a long and difficult undertaking, the success of which is not to be established by the spectator but by the conscience of the creator.

Consequently, I believe a successful work of art must have its roots deeply embedded in conviction: method and technique merely make communication possible.

As to my paving the way toward a new era in American art, I can only say that I would gladly settle for a new era for myself

I can't go along with you on the good to be gleaned from the Renaissance. The past 50 years or more have helped to break those suffocating shackles -- lets not retrogress.

I haven't seen the Guild show so will accept your statement that it lacks creative work. This situation, then, is perfectly normal. In a community such as San Diego the number of good painters is probably the same, per capita, as other communities large or small. I doubt if there is much that can be done about it. However, they are making an effort and should be commended for it. San Diego might produce another Picasso one of these days -- if so, lets hope he sidesteps naturalism.

As to my appearing as subject matter in any article you might write, I have no illusions as to my potentials and doubt very much if I could hold up as a shining example of what is needed in the world of art today.

Sincerely yours,

Mr. Alfred Wilson,
Del Mar, California.

Dear Jules:

    Here are a few observations concerning my work which might prove helpful to you in putting together your piece for the catalogue.

    As you know I am involved with an idiom which demands much of the spectator – but let me add that the painting is not intended to be "understood" in the sense that the reward is in figuring out the what it "means". On the contrary – the acceptance is in participating in the act of coming to grips with reality. My position is, therefore, to reduce to a simple composition forms that will invite interest beyond the immediate or particular – but not without cognisance of them (all phenomena exist for to the will).

    Content (not to be confused with subject matter) as such, can be no more than indications implied by the relationships of the forms and may be reflected upon by the spectator without limitation according to his capacities.

    I have struggled with this idiom for many years now + intend to pursue it further. More + more I feel an encouraging sense of achievement with it.

11.
Draft for letter to Jules Langsner from McLaughlin, 11 March 1959 (three pages, handwritten).

I know that I will never contain it because by the very nature of the undertaking the wall of resistance seems to ~~try~~ keep moving back in direct ratio to whatever sense of perception and understanding I can muster.

Obviously my objectives are in contrast to those which seek to share with the viewer an experience or idea, real or fancied, carefully planned or executed unconsciously. The notable difference is that in my case I avoid imagery or symbolism as well as the imposition of personal reflections. The reason briefly, is that to me ideas, concrete or abstract, appear as objects and consequently limit consideration to a sort of suffocating finality.

The means of implementation I have chosen are in the manipulation of neutral forms — that is the rectangle whose potential Mondrian has so ably demonstrated. I believe that forms other than rectangles assume a kind of entity and in a sense become objects and are therefore misleading. By the use of the rectangle in concert with relatively large "empty" areas I strive to create a feeling of anonymity in terms of the total canvas.

I have long been interested in Malevitch. In the Dec '58 issue of Art News P58 referring to his "Black Square on a White Ground" he is quoted as having said "the black square was by no means an empty square but the feeling of the absence of an object". This to me is a very thrilling statement and is revealing in connection with my work. Incidentally, Mondrian seems never to have gone that far but did eventually come to think in terms of "destroying the line" as well as the plane ("B'way Boogie Woogie" Etc)

For emphasis sake only: To paint the object is one thing — To paint in the knowledge that an object exists is quite another.

To conclude: "Art" then is not in the canvas but in the mind of the beholder.

Yours Etc

John

Dana Point, Mar 11 '59

17.
Compositional model for painting,
white paper on black paper, 13 x 15 in.,
ca. 1973.

Dec 7. '73

Dear Paul:

Thank you for your letter & let me say
that we would be delighted to see you
and Mrs. K at any time. Also, please
know that I appreciate your kind remarks.

As to the model — I find it indispensable
in working out compositions. I reduce it
to 1/4 scale on which I work with forms
until satisfied that it is viable and knowing
that the composition, when enlarged will
be precisely as the model. Use of the
model is also important in that I do not
risk the danger of fortuitous happenings
in composing as one paints, which in
my case would be alien to my attitude.

Again — the ease, assuredness, simplicity
and demands are essential to my work.

With kindest regards

John

13.
Letter to Paul Karlstrom, Archives of
American Art, from McLaughlin
describing use of compositional models,
7 December 1973 (one page,
handwritten).

Checklist
John McLaughlin Letters and Documents

All items in the exhibition except no. 19 are from the John McLaughlin Papers, Archives of American Art, Smithsonian Institution.

1.
Photograph of Major John McLaughlin receiving Bronze Star Medal, New Delhi, India, 5 October 1945.

2.
Letter to McLaughlin from Lawrence Sickman, curator of Oriental art, William Rockhill Nelson Gallery, Kansas City, 13 June 1947 (one page, typed).

3.
Letter to Lawrence Sickman from McLaughlin, 18 June 1947 (one page, typed).

4.
Honorable Mention ribbon for oil painting, Thirteenth Annual Festival of Arts, Laguna Beach, California, 1948.

5.
Letter to Mr. Wilson from McLaughlin, 15 January 1951 (four pages, typed) containing early statement of McLaughlin's artistic position.

6.
Letter to McLaughlin from Gordon Washburn, director, Carnegie Institute, Pittsburgh, 26 December 1951 (one page, typed).

7.
Letter to McLaughlin from Orrel P. Reed, Jr., co-director, Landau Gallery, Los Angeles, 30 December 1951 (two pages, typed).

8.
Letter to McLaughlin from Karl Benjamin, 29 August 1957 (one page, typed) containing invitation to participate in *Four Abstract Classicists* exhibition.

9.
Draft for letter to Karl Benjamin from McLaughlin, 31 August 1957 (one page, handwritten). Verso: Chinese characters for Zen and doodles.

10.
Letter to McLaughlin from Stanton Macdonald-Wright, 13 September 1958 (one page, handwritten).

11.
Draft for letter to Jules Langsner from McLaughlin, 11 March 1959 (three pages, handwritten).

12.
Letter to McLaughlin from Karl Benjamin, 29 December [1959] (first of two pages, handwritten).

13.
Letter to Paul Karlstrom, Archives of American Art, from McLaughlin describing use of compositional models, 7 December 1973 (one page, handwritten).

14.
Two photographs of McLaughlin working with compositional models, Dana Point, California, ca. 1973.

15.
Preliminary compositional sketches: ·
(a) pencil on paper, 5 x 8 in., dated May 1958. Verso: dated April 1958.
(b) pencil on lined paper, 4¼ x 5½ in., dated 17 March 1959.
(c) pencil on green paper, 6¼ x 4 in. undated.

16.
Compositional model for painting, black paper on white paper, 13 x 15 in., ca. 1973.

17.
Compositional model for painting, white paper on black paper, 13 x 15 in., ca. 1973.

18.
Composition, oil sketch on paper (fragment), 5¾ x 5¼ in., undated.

19.
Photograph of McLaughlin by John Waggaman.

Photograph Credits:

Los Angeles County Museum of Art: 5, 11, 13, 17.
John Waggaman: 19.

5.

Environmental Communications Looks at Los Angeles

Southern California constitutes one vast garden, cut up into a world of Edens. Oscar Schuck, *The California Scrapbook,* New York, 1869. Quotation unearthed by David Gebhard.

L.A. is Truth—whether you like it or not.
> Louis Kahn, 1972, at the Aspen Design Conference, in an evening of Kahn and Environmental Communications.

An important discovery of Surrealists and advertisers has been that man responds to and remembers that which is inappropriate.
> Charles Jencks, in *Architectural Design,* September 1973.

COUNCIL KILLS TIGHTER RULES ON BILLBOARDS
Rejection of Braude Ordinance Climaxes 6-Year Controversy

While conceding that billboards are "not the prettiest things in the world," Councilman Zev Yaroslavsky maintained that "they have a very important contribution to make to the community and various organizations." He drew laughter when he observed that "half of the people around this table aren't pretty either, but we don't zone them."
> from the *Los Angeles Times*

Two of Los Angeles' unwritten civic ordinances: success is transitory, and change is inevitable.
> John Pastier

I like most of the streets where the houses go all the way from Gothic to International style, rambling on and on for block after block with what appears to some people pure anonymity, but what appears to me to be an exciting fantasyland to wander through. If you go to Bel-Air you can see it at the million-dollar level, and if you go to Culver City you can see it at the twenty-one thousand-dollar level. But the fantasy is essentially the same.
> Roland Coate

Neon in a pure state is a magical drawing material. We think of medieval manuscript illuminations transformed into reality, of the crackling sci-fi apparatus of Dr. Frankenstein's laboratory. We see colors that put color-field painting to shame.
> William Wilson
> *Los Angeles Times*
> 9 March 1973

Rudolph Schindler and Los Angeles are one and inseparable. Until Los Angeles was (reluctantly) seen as the city of the present it was impossible to sense what Schindler was about. In turn Los Angeles could not be discovered until the fashion for the International style and formal city planning was no longer stylish or "smart." Complexity, ambiguity, contradiction are the ingredients of Schindler's architecture, just as they are the guts and substance of the new city. Planning, visual and non-visual, can only exist in fragments, not as a whole. This is what Schindler's architecture is all about.
> David Gebhard
> *Schindler,* New York, 1971

Environmental Communications is a small group of Los Angeles photographers, videotapers, researchers, and editors operating under the direction of David Greenberg. It was founded in 1969, in Greenberg's words, "out of disappointment in the lack of relevance of the architectural education process and the direction of the architectural discipline." Greenberg, newly graduated from Arizona State University with a degree of bachelor in architecture, was deeply struck by three technological developments of the late sixties, new photographic tools that could "perceive and create a near infinite amount of perspective within a few minutes." In 1967 the Pentax single lens reflex 35 mm camera was introduced; a year later the Beaulieu Super-8 movie camera was marketed; and in 1969 Sony made available the one-half inch black and white videotape Port-a-pak. An architect now had the capacity of a "third eye": he could instantly change focal length, simultaneously studying the environmental context to which the building would be related.

Greenberg commented that "in the 19th century the built forms in a city were perceived by a populace averaging a foot speed of about 2½ mph. In recent times Angelenos have been perceiving their built environment at an average speed of about 50 mph." The architectural profession, he felt, was insufficiently dealing with this factor, and was encouraging retrograde designs for dwellings while ignoring the new visual fabric of the environment. The thrust of EC was to sensitize people to what already lay before their eyes. The special urgency one feels in their work is reflected in comments such as EC photographer Roger Webster's: *To drive across town without my camera can be very painful. And, L.A. is a flat automotive circus and you photograph it while driving through it, you use your knees not your hands to drive, your teeth if necessary—you give the controls to the passenger, even if he is in the back seat. You abandon the car at stop lights. You ignore traffic regulations. You risk your life.*

Greenberg anticipates the installation at LACMA as follows:

> A 45-minute color and black and white video cassette player hooked up to two television monitors and electronically beeping instructions to a programmer dissolving at various speeds with 162 slides from two slide projectors placed behind an 8 x 12 foot vinyl screen set into a 2 x 4 inch stud wall built floor to ceiling (12 feet high) and across the 20 x 30 foot gallery space at 130° angle.

We are especially pleased to present here a new essay, "Chester Gould versus Roy Lichtenstein," by writer **Tom Wolfe**. A Ph. D. in American Studies at Yale, Wolfe has revolutionized the style of American journalism with his early attention to matters of lifestyle that everyone talked about but no one wrote about. He is the author of *The Kandy-Kolored Tangerine Flake Streamline Baby,* 1965; *The Kool-Aid Acid Test,* 1968; and the *Painted Word,* 1975. Much of his writing concerns Los Angeles, including an article on *electrographic architecture* published in the Los Angeles Times' *West* magazine. His new book, *Mauve Gloves & Madmen, Clutter & Vine* was recently published by Farrar, Straus and Giroux.

M. T.

2 3

4 5

6

1924

Chester Gould Versus Roy Lichtenstein

Tom Wolfe

Frankly, I would like to see the term *popular culture* disappear from the language. It never fails to bring darkness and gibberish down upon anyone who tries to use it. Once a visual phenomenon is categorized as part of popular culture, this is a signal to everyone in the art world that it is not necessary to take it seriously, although one is perfectly free to enjoy it in the spirit of Camp or nostalgia for the mud. This was precisely the spirit of Pop art. The Pop artists operated on the level of Carl van Vechten visiting Harlem in the 1920s and writing *Nigger Heaven.* Warhol, Lichtenstein, Oldenburg, Indiana, and the rest brought back comic strip panels, Campbell Soup cans, Brillo boxes, Rexall drug store boys' first basemen's mitts, and neon signs in the spirit of anthropologists returning with tribal masks. They were capturing the world of high culture the icons created by energetic but unsophisticated and nameless artisans who did commercial designs for the populace . . . out there. It was on this point, however — namely, sophistication — that Pop Art ran into problems.

Too often the artisans whose work the Pop artists adapted or copied were not unsophisticated (nor, for that matter, nameless). I can remember a show that Andy Warhol and several artists put on at the old Bianchini Gallery in New York. It was called *Supermarket,* and they attempted to turn the interior of the gallery into a sophisticated version of the fluorescent glare and serial repetition (of packages, apples, cauliflowers, bottles, and so on) of a supermarket. The result was something curiously pallid, however, and the show sank without a bubble. In fact, the show itself was *unsophisticated.* By the 1960s supermarket interiors were being put together by highly sophisticated designers and electrical engineers whose aims were rather similar to an artist's:

originality, surprise, impact, careful (even if bizarre) combinations of light and color, and stimulation of the unconscious. When it came to creating a sculptural interior using electric light and the serial repetition of forms, they knew more than Warhol and his associates and were more expert in using the available materials and techniques. In short, they were more sophisticated.

One has only to compare the comic strip pictures of Chester Gould (*Dick Tracy*) with those of Lichtenstein to see the same point illustrated. When it comes to the decisive use of line, when it comes to combining chiaroscuro and blocs of primary colors in two dimensions (perspective is of little use in the small space of a comic strip panel), Gould is more expert and more sophisticated than Lichtenstein. This is not meant as negative statement about Lichtenstein, whose work I personally enjoy (although not so much as Gould's). After all, Gould has had far more experience. In any event, where Gould excels, it is as an artist and not as a purveyor of "popular culture." Once, while driving along an elevated stretch of the Santa Monica Freeway in Los Angeles at dusk, I was struck by the sight of the thousands of glowing objects that seemed to float above the landscape. Most of these were electric signs or symbols that were stuck up in the air on standards precisely so they could be seen from automobiles. The most striking of all, it seemed to me, were the orange and blue UNION 76 balls revolving like big lit-up basketballs over service stations all over the city.

Somehow a vast electric orange ball galaxy had been created forty feet above the Los Angeles basin. I set about what I figured would be the difficult search to find out what nameless and unsophisticated artisan had inadvertently succeeded in creating his own starscape over L. A. in this fashion. His name turned out to be Raymond Loewy. Raymond Loewy is probably the best-known commercial designer in America. Very little that Raymond Loewy does is inadvertent. He had thought out "Floating Electric Orange and Blue Basketballs Over Los Angeles" down to the last watt of light and inch of elevation. Again, I have personally enjoyed the work of many serious artists who have tried to take art out into "the environment" in a big way. But I would urge all of them, even Christo, to spend a year at the knee of Raymond Loewy, to learn from him not as Loewy the technician but as Loewy the artist.

During the 1960s art-minded friends of mine used to like to point out, with great Pop Cult delight, certain gasoline stations in Los Angeles, and especially the Union 76 station in Beverly Hills at Santa Monica Boulevard and Crescent Drive. This station looks like some sort of Futurama Pagoda. Actually it is a huge spherical triangle resting on three piers with curving soffits lined with fluorescent strips of color. It turned out to be by another well-known designer, Jim Wong of Pereira Associates. What Wong has done here with electric-light sculpture — as an artist — goes so far beyond what serious light sculptors like Billy Apple and Dan Flavin (and serious architects, for that matter) have yet attempted; it poses a serious question for art historians.

I would like to make the modest suggestion that in most areas of contemporary art, commercial designers are now a good decade ahead of serious (i.e. fashionable) artists — as artists — and if we are serious about art history we will record their names as their work pops up in the amazing tableaux of Los Angeles and other American cities...and will not consign them to the oblivion of popular culture. The very term Popular culture has unconsciously become a wall protecting serious art from the competition of the more sophisticated and gifted creatures, the platinum huns, as it were, in the...world out there...

One has only to compare the comic strip pictures of Chester Gould (*Dick Tracy*) with those of Lichtenstein to see the same point illustrated. When it comes to the decisive use of line, when it comes to combining chiaroscuro and blocs of primary colors in two dimensions (perspective is of little use in the small space of a comic strip panel), Gould is more expert and more sophisticated than Lichtenstein. This is not meant as negative statement about Lichtenstein, whose work I personally enjoy (although not so much as Gould's). After all, Gould has had far more experience. In any event, where Gould excels, it is as an artist and not as a purveyor of "popular culture." Once, while driving along an elevated stretch of the Santa Monica Freeway in Los Angeles at dusk, I was struck by the sight of the thousands of glowing objects that seemed to float above the landscape. Most of these were electric signs or symbols that were stuck up in the air on standards precisely so they could be seen from automobiles. The most striking of all, it seemed to me, were the orange and blue UNION 76 balls revolving like big lit-up basketballs over service stations all over the city.

8

The Santa Monica/San Diego intersection
is a work of art, both as a pattern on the map,
as a monument against the sky, and as a
kinetic experience as one sweeps through it.

Reyner Banham,
Los Angeles: The Architecture of Four Ecologies.

10

11

13

12

If we can make our urban envi: classrooms with endless windo

14

16

18

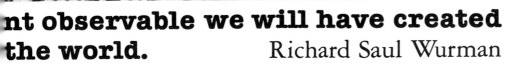

nt observable we will have created
the world.   Richard Saul Wurman

15

8

19

20

21

They were very fussy about the quality of the meat as it would appear on the billboard. They wanted it to look alive and not dead. But if it looked alive with too many highlights it would look greasy. The greatest concern was to make it look appetizing.

Glen Johnson, art director of Foster & Kle on the subject of the MacDonald's hamburger billb

22

27

3

Traditions inherited from the ranch period (early nineteenth century) encouraged a tendency to "speak in superlatives, to live out-of-doors tell tall tales, to deal in real estate, to believe what isn't true, to thro dignity out the window, to dress dramatically and, last but not least, tackle the impossible.

Reyner Banham, *Los Angeles: The Architecture of Four Ecol*

24

25

26

28 29

30

31

38

37

32

Our senses include vision, hearing, smell, touch and temperature, but scientific findings indicate that we receive about 90 percent of our information through sight.

Los Angeles Department of City Planning,
The Visual Environment of Los Angeles, April 1971.

34

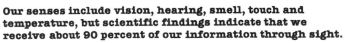

33

35

36

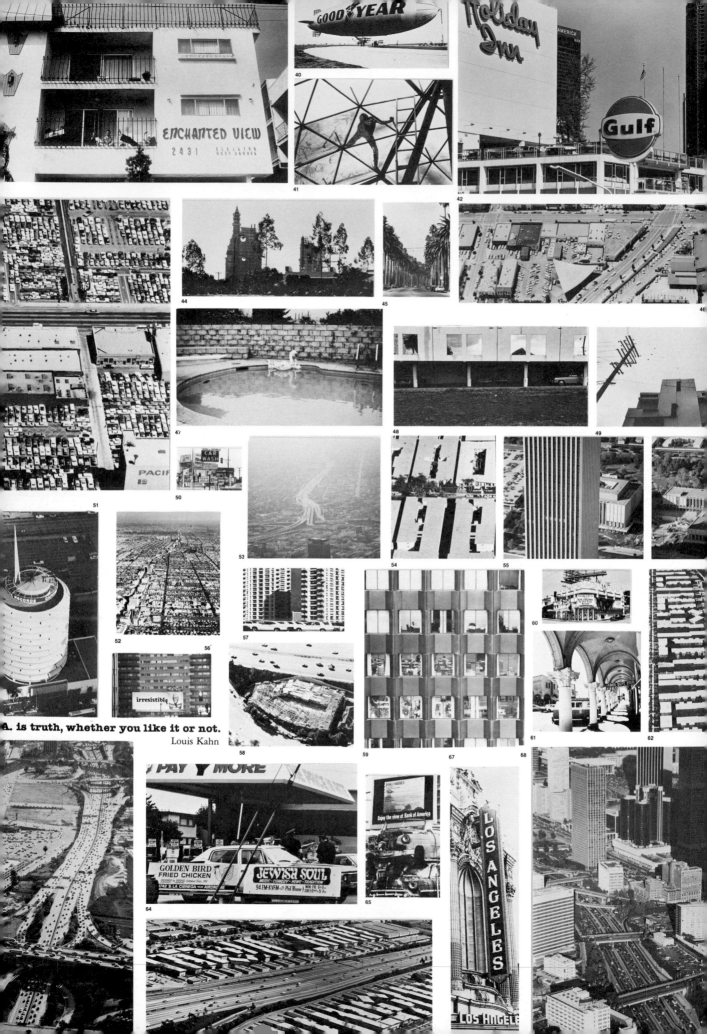

A. is truth, whether you like it or not.
Louis Kahn

69 73 70 71 74 72

76 77 79 81

75 82 83 78 80

84 85 86 87 89

90 91 96

92 93 94 95

98 100

CALIFORNIA FEDERAL

Then the building (shaped like a piano) — was sold to the refrigeration equipment company. The 150-foot-long showroom displayed scales and freezer cases instead of pianos on its three-tiered terraced floor, but the piano entrance remained intact. Perhaps that was its finest hour as an art work. Stripped commercial practicality and literal symbolism, it was now a pie of pure sculpture.

John Pastier, *Los Angeles Times*, July 2,

Environmental Communications: What about the Sanka coffee "Indulge Yourself" Campaign?

Glen Johnson, art director of Foster & Kleiser: We took dummie (fiberglass) and broke their arms and legs to get them into the right positions. We used a plastic fabric to cover the material of their clothing so it would stand up under weather conditions. Regular fabric would have deteriorated too fast.

E. C.: You mean they were not painted but were real mannequin

Johnson: Oh, yes, there were about eight different settings. One was dipping a ladle into the cup, one was on stilts, one was a mountaineer, etc. Each time they would rotate them into UCLA they would have to put up another dummy, as the kids would rip them off. No matter how high we would put them up they would take it as a game to try and get them down.

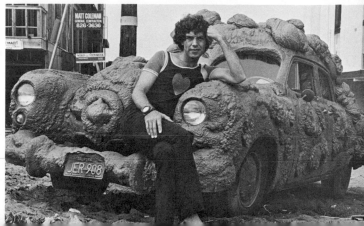

107

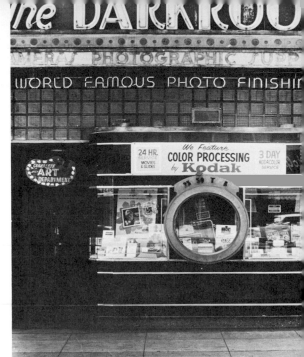

108

109

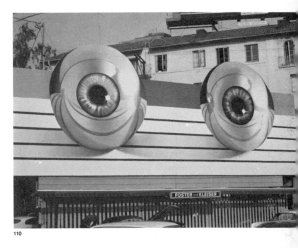

110

111

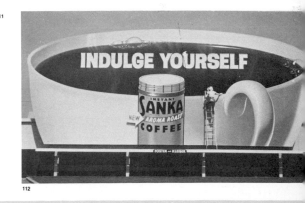

112

114

The works on these two pages are by Hideko Kambe, a young Japanese artist living in Los Angeles. In her art she uses the photographic medium to compose near-equal parts of handpainted billboards and the Los Angeles environment surrounding them.

119

120

121

122

123

Smart women
cook with
modern GAS

FOSTER •• KLEISER

124

125

CAPITOL REC

126

127

HOLLYW

COOL-

128

GOOD

**The
Concept:**

Basically, the laboratory/studio is LOS ANGELES. The o
viewpoint involves defining it as a changing "creative"
thetic experience, and seeing it as a quasi-living ORGA

The challenge of course is the attempt to describe it in
istic manner, as well as focusing in on specific, re-occ

129

FOODS

131 132

133

cultural phenomena — isolating individual
...ensional artifacts like a billboard, a space,
...ng, an area. In fact, the entire Greater Los
...Area is viewed as a composition of inter-
...orms, of artifacts creating an amorphous,
...nging MEGARTIFACT: L.A.

134

135

137

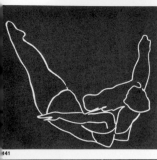

Psychiatrist
EASY TERMS

140

141

139

BAKERY

142

144

SHRIMP

143

THE
HOT DOG SHOW

145

NEON

146

SIGN

146

PEP

147

148

149

CLAYTON
PLUMBERS

McDon
HAMBUF
OVER

Delicate glass lariats of light are scribbled like enchanted frosting across the nightime face of the city . . . neon is the magic wand that gives downtown its nervous boogie-woogie spirit, etching edges of buildings embroidering tapestries of light across movie palace marquees.

William Wilson,
Los Angeles Times,
9 March 1973.

THE HOT DOG.. SHOW

The French scientist George Claude built the first neon sign in Paris in 1921. The Eiffel Tower was outlined in neon in 1926. In 1928 California claimed the largest concentration of electric signs in the country.

STANDARD

Neon is the fifth most prevalent element in the universe.

Carl Sagen
Intelligent Life In The Universe

153

155

156

1. "A while back we got a number of complaints from the residents…they said there were rats in the palm trees." So the city decided on an experiment. "We got a bunch of aluminum bands and fastened the[m] around the trunks. This discouraged the rodents for about as long as it took them to discover the telephone poles along the sam[e] street. They simply climbed the poles and used the telephone cables as a freeway system to the palms.   *Los Angeles Tim[es]*

2. Down the aisle sits "Peaches and Creme," a 1934 Ford coupe with a 1968 Corvette engine and a body painted "campus creme" on top and "bronze starflake" below (and a sign: Do Not Touch This Car Unless You are Completely Nude!). Nearby a crowd is gathering in front of the "Archie Bunker Hard Hat Hauler." The Hauler features a lunch-bucket gas tank, a chromed hard-hat roof.   *Time Magazine* review of t[he] 1973 Custom Car Show, March 197[3]

3. Our objective was to supply specification[s] that would conform to the engineering standards of a 50 mile an hour curve, while making it as aesthetically pleasing as possible.   Marilyn Reese, Project Designer of t[he] Santa Monica/San Diego interchan[ge]

4. The shadow of a Watts Tower.
I no have anybody to help me out. I was a poor man. Had to do a little at a time. Nobo[dy] helped me. I think if I hire a man he don't know what to do. A million times I don't know what to do myself. I never had a sing[le] helper. Some of the people say what was he doing…some of the people think I was cra[zy] and some people said I was going to do something. I wanted to do something in the United States because I was raised here. Yo[u] understand? I wanted to do something for the United States because there are nice people in this country.   Simon Rod[ia] designer/builder, Watts Tow[er]

157

158

159

160

162

the highest, most logical, purest and most powerful type of painting is mural painting...it cannot be converted into an object of personal gain nor can it be concealed for the benefit of a few privileged people. It is for the people.

Jose Clemente Orozco, Mexican muralist, 1929.

161

"Do all of you write your names on the walls?"
"Sure! Except him."
"Don't you write?"
"No, I don't write!"
"Why Not?"
"I got somebody who writes for me."

Norman Mailer, *The Faith of Graffiti,* Praeger Publishers, New York, 1974.

163

164

The works on this page are all street paintings done by the Los Angeles Fine Arts Squad. The group was formed around spring 1969 in an effort to create an alternative to the "La Cienega Society." Quite logically, they turned to the street and began painting the brick wall outside the studio-residence of Terry Schoonhaven (one of the members of the L.A.F.A.S.) on Brooks Street in Venice. The result was a precise, mirrored

165

166

167

168

169

reflection in deep perspective of the view down Brooks which faced the painting. This "mirror image" is still intact.
The other members of the group included Vic Henderson, Leonard Koren, and Jim Frazen. Terry Schoonhaven is painting alone now, still using the name of the Los Angeles Fine Arts Squad.
These are really paintings in the oldest sense. They're stories, a high amount of idea content in a kind of theatrical way, an illusionistic theatrical way. We have no interest in experimenting with surfaces or with abstractions of shape and form.

Terry Schoonhaven

170

That place on La Cienega is such an awful building. What they managed to do was to make it disappear. In certain light, their sky blends with the real sky and the building just goes poof.

Larry Bell speaking about *The Beverly Hills Siddhartha* on the walls of the Climax Club.

I have no objection to painted buildings as long as they are privately owned and away from the street — I am not enthusiastic about it.

Art Oplinger, coordinator, Los Angeles Municipal Arts Commission, speaking about *The Beverly Hills Siddhartha*.

171

172

174

173   175

176

178

179   177

180   181

Los Angeles, without its people and its cars and its activity, will make a lousy ruin.

Architectural Record, August 1976

182

You are plugged into an endless, beginningless stream (Where does the damn thing start anyway?) of herded, lacquered metal that, ordinarily friendly, can turn vicious on you, thundering towards indefinable ends. You are thrown together laterally on the freeway, and always bothered by those keeping the same speed as you; it's a blockade if you're in a hurry trying to weave between the shuffling buffaloes. You seem a daredevil Kamikaze if you go any slower.

Walter Gabrielson, *Architectural Design*, September 1973.

If motorway driving anywhere calls for a high level of attentiveness, the extreme concentration required in Los Angeles seems to bring on a state of heightened awareness that some locals find mystical.

Reyner Banham, *Los Angeles: The Architecture of Four Ecologies*   Penguin Press.

185

187   188

Notes

1. View north on Main Street from P.S. Building, 1907. Photograph courtesy of Title Insurance and Trust Company.
2. Panorama from 9th and Main Streets. Looking north on Spring and Main Streets, 1917. Photograph courtesy of Title Insurance and Trust Company.
3. Rogers Airport looking east from Wilshire and San Vicente Boulevards, 1921. Photograph courtesy of Spence Aerial Collection.
4. Aerial photograph of Westwood, 1930. Photograph courtesy of Spence Air Photos.
5. View northeast of 8th and Hope Streets with Navy Airship *Akron* in the foreground, 1932. Photograph courtesy of Spence Air Photos.
6. Santa Monica and Wilshire Boulevards, 1924. Photograph courtesy of Spence Air Photos.
7. Close-up of Union 76 ball with a coffee shop parking lot reflected. Photograph Roger Webster, 1973.
8. & 9. Two views of the Santa Monica/San Diego Freeway interchange, designed and built 1959-1963. The interchange won the Governor's Design Award. The head designer was Marilyn Reese. Photograph 1976.
10. View north to the famous Hollywood sign with the Beachwood section of the Hollywood Hills below.
11. The San Diego Freeway with the Wilshire Boulevard eastbound off-ramp. Intersection below is Wilshire and Sepulveda Boulevards.
12. View west of City Hall in the foreground with the Civic Center Mall directly behind. The mall leads to the Music Center and the Department of Water and Power Building. 1971.
13. Sunset Boulevard at Crescent Heights Boulevard. Next to the pie-shaped wedge is the original Schwab's Drug Store. The concrete wedge in the lower righthand corner was once the site of Pandora's Box, a gathering place in the early sixties for long-haired "hippies." 1976.
14. The Hollywood Hills with lots of cliff-hangers. 1976.
15. View south along the San Diego Freeway at the Wilshire Boulevard off-ramp. The Veterans Administration Hospital is in the upper righthand corner.
16. View east of Wilshire Boulevard as it curves around MacArthur (Westlake) Park. In the foreground is the reflective CNA Building.
17. View southwest in Hollywood. The half golfball shape of the Hollywood Cinerama Dome is to the left. The building in the right foreground with the American Airlines sign marks the famous intersection of Hollywood and Vine. 1971.
18. Panorama of the Santa Monica Freeway. The view is from the beginning of the freeway at Santa Monica beach eastward toward downtown Los Angeles. In the middle photograph is Main Street behind the Holiday Inn as it runs past the Santa Monica courthouse. In the bottom photograph is the Santa Monica Pier and Palisades Park with its cannon.
18. Billboard on Sunset Strip announcing pornographic film, *Defiance,* 1976.
19. Foster & Kleiser billboard artist painting a sesame seed on a Big Mac.
20. Example of what Dr. Robert Winter calls "belly-button" architecture. Dingbat resident peering over the belly button of an apartment on Beverly Glen Boulevard, West Los Angeles. (The term "dingbat" refers to minimal multi-family housing.)
21. Billboard on the side of the Whiskey-A-Go-Go, Sunset Strip, announcing the Steve Miller Band's latest album, 1974.
22. Miscellaneous commercial graphics, downtown Los Angeles.
23. Billboard, Sunset Strip, Los Angeles.
24. Lincoln Boulevard, 1974, Venice.
25. Wall painting on offices of A&M Records, La Cienega Boulevard, Los Angeles.
26. Billboard, atop Music City, Hollywood.
27. Man standing in front of typical urban clutter, downtown Los Angeles. Photography by John Bright.
28. Nightclub graphics, Sunset Strip and Larabee Street, West Hollywood. Billboard for "Dollars" a film.
29. Two-story bottle of "the real thing," Coca-Cola Bottling Plant, East Los Angeles.
30. Ubiquitous Union 76 ball, rush hour, Sunset Boulevard and Highland Avenue, Hollywood.
31. Santa Monica Boulevard car wash franchise.
32. Two-story fiberglass tire salesman, innovation of International Fiberglass, Los Angeles.
33. Lincoln Boulevard, Venice.
34. View of Los Angeles City Hall, downtown Los Angeles. Photograph by Roger Webster.
35. Santa Monica Boulevard center divider, West Los Angeles.
36. Billboard announcing album of rock group War, West Hollywood.
37. Billboard row, Santa Monica Boulevard center divider, West Los Angeles.
38. Los Angeles Theatre. Photograph by David Greenberg, 1968.
39. Dingbat apartment in Santa Monica, 1972.
40. Goodyear blimp "Columbia" at blimp base in Carson, 1971.
41. Man applying mylar on geodesic dome designed by Bernard Judge. Originally built on Beachwood Drive in the Hollywood Hills, it is now dismantled and stored at the Smithsonian Institution, Washington, D.C. The dome was constructed in 1961.
42. Holiday Inn near Convention Center, downtown Los Angeles.
43. Aerial photograph of downtown Los Angeles.
44. 20th Century Fox Studios as seen from Century City. Backdrop scenery is from the film *Hello Dolly.*
45. Typical palm-lined street in Beverly Hills.
46. Detail from aerial photograph of Santa Monica Boulevard and Canon Drive in Beverly Hills. The triangular shape in the center is a Union 76 station designed by Jim Wong of Pereira Associates.
47. Swimming pool in the backyard of an Encino home. Photograph by Roger Webster.
48. View of the back of a Los Angeles apartment building, 1976. Photograph by John Samargis.
49. Lovell Beach House, Newport Beach, California, designed by Rudolph Schindler and built in 1926. Photograph by Roger Webster.
50. Sign clutter in downtown Los Angeles. Photo by Roger Webster.
51. Capitol Records Tower, Vine Street, Hollywood. Designed by Welton Becket to look like a stack of records and built in 1956, this round building was said to be a safe place for young women to work because their bosses couldn't "corner" them.
52. Wilshire Boulevard "corridor" in 1969 looking east toward the downtown area.
53. Harbor/Santa Monica Freeway interchange. Occidental Tower at bottom was headlined on November 19, 1976 as Los Angeles' "Towering Inferno" because a fire broke out on the upper floors. This photograph by Ron Cooper was taken approximately ten days before the fire.
54. Aerial photograph of apartment buildings in the San Fernando Valley north of Los Angeles.
55. Two views of the Los Angeles County Museum of Art, 1976, taken a fraction of a second apart. Photographs by Ron Cooper.
56. Barrington Plaza apartment buildings on Barrington Avenue and Wilshire Boulevard in West Los Angeles. The architect is anonymous.
57. Apartment buildings in Century City.
58. Apartment building under construction near the San Fernando Valley section of the San Diego Freeway, 1971. The shape of the building relates to the adjacent freeway and the roads around it.

59. Closeup view into a Century City office building.

60. Whisky-A-Go-Go on the Sunset Strip at Clark Street. Photograph by Roger Webster.

61. Windward Avenue in Venice looking toward the beach. The offices of Environmental Communications are on the far side of picture.

62. UCLA graduate student housing next to the San Diego Freeway near the Santa Monica interchange. The State Division of Highways (now Caltrans) conducted a survey in the sixties to find out how people felt about living next to freeways. Three out of four didn't mind at all.

63. The original, classic four-level interchange in downtown Los Angeles, 1976 photograph.

64. Robertson Boulevard south of Pico Boulevard.

65. Two cars being taken to the wrecking yard.

66. UCLA graduate student housing next to the San Diego Freeway.

67. Los Angeles Theater on South Broadway in downtown Los Angeles.

68. Looking east on the Harbor Freeway. The round cluster of buildings is the Bonaventure Hotel, opening in 1977.

69. Cliff-hanging apartment in hills overlooking Playa del Rey Beach, 1971.

70. Marlboro Man billboard on San Diego Freeway near Compton.

71. Palm trees on the horizon.

72. Old apartment building on 6th Street near Alvarado Street.

73. Billboard on Sunset Boulevard.

74. Aerial view of City Hall surrounded by county office buildings, 1976.

75. Aerial view of the San Diego and Nixon Freeways leading to Marina del Rey. The Nixon Freeway was never officially dedicated because of President Richard M. Nixon's resignation. The *Los Angeles Times* referred to the freeway as the shortest and most dangerous freeway in the world that doesn't go anywhere.

76. Acres of parked cars.

77. Traveling east on Wilshire Boulevard at the beginning of the Miracle Mile.

78. Big Donut Drive-In.

79. Handpainted billboard.

80. Handpainted billboard. Photograph by Foster & Kleiser. Early sixties.

81. Harbor Freeway eastbound in downtown Los Angeles, 1971.

82. A classic Los Angeles sunset, complete with red flaming sky and palm trees, as seen from Sunset Boulevard and Fairfax Avenue.

83. Aerial view of the Hollywood Cinerama Dome.

84. Aerial view of Century City. The twenty-story Century City Hotel is dwarfed by the twin triangle towers designed by Minoru Yamasaki in 1974.

85. The Hollywood Cinerama Dome with Los Angeles First Federal Savings and Loan in the background.

86. Disneyland train station with Mickey's face in front.

87. CNA Building designed by Langdon and Wilson in 1972 reflects church across the street. The location is Wilshire Boulevard near the downtown area.

88. Westwood Village in 1969 when there were only three high-rise buildings in the area. Photograph by David Greenberg.

89. Santa Monica and Wilshire Boulevards at the edge of Beverly Hills.

90. A traffic circle replete with palm trees within the Park La Brea Towers.

91. Yards and yards of flags attracting attention to a car lot on Sunset Strip.

92. Typical row of dingbat housing in Los Angeles.

93. Piles of junked cars about to be flattened into smaller piles of metal which will be reincarnated eventually into the latest automobile model, among other things.

94. Los Angeles clutter.

95. Harbor/Santa Monica Freeway interchange looking north.

96. Aerial view of downtown Los Angeles. City Hall is no longer the tallest building in the area, and is surrounded by other government buildings.

97. Aerial view of downtown Los Angeles looking southeast. The Department of Water and Power Building is to the left with the Music Center behind it.

98. This billboard refers to Lake Arrowhead, not Los Angeles.

99. Downtown aerial view.

100. Aerial view of Park La Brea Towers. Wilshire Boulevard separates it from California Federal Savings.

101. Giant Texaco men (1963), dinosaurs (1966), tiger, and semi-truck, Venice. International Fiberglass.

102. Posters from the "Smart Women Cook with Gas" campaign of the Southern California Gas Company being handpainted. This was one of the first handpainted billboard campaigns used in Los Angeles by Foster & Kleiser.

103. Manning's Big Red Piano Shop, Venice Boulevard, 1930. Frank H. Gaw was the architect. Part of the adjoining structure was destroyed by fire in 1972, and the Department of Building and Safety ruled that the piano shop was part of the structure that had burned and could not be left standing. The owner of the piano shop building offered it to anyone who would take it, and finally Tom Sewell offered to move it to Venice. In June 1973, as it was being resettled twelve miles west of its original location, the unsupported structure broke apart and crashed to the ground.

104. Billboard advertising Frank Zappa's movie *200 Motels*. Designed by Craig Butler.

105. Ferrocement dinosaur in Cabazon. Designed by Claude Bell, the dinosaur took almost twelve years to build and cost more than $500,000. It is now open to the public as a museum; for 25 cents you can walk through it and see painted cavemen and bas relief heads depicting the story of the first man.

106. Tom Sewell sitting on his "Pickle Mobile," a Studebaker sprayed with polyurethane foam and painted pickle green.

107. Handpainted billboard advertising a rock album on the Sunset Strip across from Ciro's nightclub.

108. Camera shop, Wilshire Boulevard, 1938.

109. People sitting on bus stop benches in front of the Bank of America on Hollywood Boulevard.

110. A billboard for the rock opera album "Tommy" on the Sunset Strip, 1972.

111. This modified 1959 Cadillac hearse was designed and built by Señor Jitanos, a recent immigrant from Spain who had been a wood craftsman, and his son. It is an example of "nomadic truckitecture." "We now knew we had the power to make independent choices about our lives. Examples of this independent thinking which immediately sprung up are the cultural mutants mentioned earlier, the nomadic truckitects. Nomadic truckitecture is a term coined by Environmental Communications, a Los Angeles group. The term describes a primarily West Coast development in mobile living—the remodeling and creative redesigning of vehicles for living on the road." From "A Trip Down U.S. Highways from World War II to the Future," by Ant Farm, *Automerica*, E.P. Dutton, New York.

112. Indulge Yourself Billboard by Foster & Kleiser. One of a series.

113. Detail from car at the custom car show Los Angeles.

114. Standard Station and Billboard. West Hollywood, 1971.

115-121. Hideko Kambe

122. Detail from Coppertone billboard, 1969.

123. Handpainted billboard, one of a series of "Smart Women." Photo courtesy of Foster & Kleiser.

124. Tail o' Pup hot dog stand, La Cienega Boulevard near Beverly Boulevard, Beverly Hills.

125. Capitol Records Tower on Vine Street above Hollywood Boulevard, Hollywood. 25' sculptures stand atop during Christmas holidays, 1974.

126. Coca-Cola Bottling Plant, 1915. As the company grew, more buildings were constructed, but no unifying design existed. Therefore, the Barbee Brothers, who owned the plant, hired Robert Derrah in 1935 to create one. He constructed a ship shape which enclosed the other buildings within it. In June 1976, it became the city's historical monument number 138.

127. Billboard photograph by Hideko Kambe.

128. The Goodyear blimp "Columbia" on television. Environmental Communications has used the blimp to get many of its aerial photographs and video time-lapse material.

129. A billboard in front of a cooling tower at the end of the Pasadena Freeway. Photograph by David Greenberg.

130. Christopher Columbus Transcontinental Highway (formerly the Santa Monica Freeway) and Harbor Freeway interchange near downtown Los Angeles.

131. Victorian house, downtown Los Angeles. Photograph by Virgil Mirano.

132. Photograph taken from the Goodyear blimp "Columbia" showing smog filling the Los Angeles basin and surrounding hills.

133. Goodyear blimp.

134. Aerial view of the remains of the Venice Canals, 1970. The canals were originally designed in 1904 as part of the Venice real estate development project conceived and executed primarily by Abbott Kinney. The canal network originally

stretched from what is now the Marina Del Rey peninsula to Brooks Street. When Venice became part of the City of Los Angeles all the canals except these were paved over.

135. Union 76 ball, Hollywood.

136. Anonymous mobile home park.

137. Felix the Cat, Felix Chevrolet, Figueroa Street and Exposition Boulevard, Los Angeles. Winslow B. Felix opened the car dealership in December 1921. Pat Sullivan, the originator of the *Felix the Cat* cartoon strip, gave Felix permission to use the cat in a sign on top of the original location at 12th Street and Grand Avenue. The present owner, Nich Shamus, was able to get permission to place the fifteen-foot Felix at the Figueroa location—the sign, by today's standards, would be impossible to put up because of legal prohibitions against large signs facing freeways.

138. RCA Victor, from the *Neon Signs & Symbols* exhibit at California State College, Fullerton, 1973. The sign is 100 inches high and twenty-two inches wide.

139. Bruin Theater marquee, Westwood, 1970.

140. Miscellaneous neon, Los Angeles.

141. Diving Lady, Johnson Pool Company, Chatsworth.

142. Bakery, Fairfax Avenue, Los Angeles.

143. Air Lane Restaurant, Wilshire Boulevard, Santa Monica, 1939.

144. Motorcycle from the Los Angeles Custom Car Show, 1973

145. Hot Dog Show, La Cienega and Beverly Boulevards, Los Angeles, ca. 1940.

146. Neon Sign, from *Neon Signs & Symbols.*

147. PEP, from *Neon Signs & Symbols.* The sign is twenty-one feet wide and eight feet high and was constructed by Advance Electric Sign Company, Los Angeles.

148. First Generation MacDonald's Neon Golden Arches, ca. mid-1960s.

149. Clayton Plumbing, Westwood Boulevard, Westwood.

150. Electrical Storm over Los Angeles, view from the Hollywood Hills, summer 1976. Time exposure photograph by Jurg Victor Walther.

151. The Hot Dog Show, La Cienega and Beverly Boulevards, ca. 1940s.

152. Standard Gas station sign, Los Angeles.

153. Palm trees in Los Angeles. The average fan palm grows approximately sixty feet. Although they have no rings, they are believed to be among the most durable trees.

154. Two billboards near Beverly Hills. Photography by Susan Sullivan, 1975.

155. A wide-angle view of the Custom Car Show at the Sports Arena in 1973.

156. Aerial photograph of Santa Monica/San Diego Freeway interchange.

157. Watts Towers. (Detail)

158. Bob's Big Boy, The Valley. Photography by Susan Sullivan.

159. Mickey Mouse mural in Astrada Courts, East Los Angeles, by Carlito Gaegos.

160. Alley mural in East Los Angeles by Willie Herron.

161. "Compas Place" on Rosecrans Boulevard in Norwalk provides the format for individual "calling cards" and gang *plaqueasos.* (Street writers call their graffiti *placas* or *plaqueasos.* The Spanish word *placa* means a plaque or a sign and is used interchangeably with the slang *plaqueaso.*)

162. This alley mural in East Los Angeles by artist Willie Herron was a 1972 independent project of the artist. The mural stands in an alley near East City Terrace Drive and North Miller Avenue.

163. Mural in East Los Angeles showing a group of seated men with an Aztec Indian on the right and a Spanish conquistador in the background. On the left, hidden behind a bush, is a revolutionary with bullet belts slung across his chest. Artist unknown.

164. This death skull mural on City Terrace stairway of Eastern Avenue and Comly Drive was a 1972 independent project of "La Regeneracion," a group of artists consisting of Willie Herron, Patsy Valdez, Gronk, and Harry Gamboa.

165. Detail from *Venice in Snow,* also known as *The Ocean Front Painting,* 1970. The person depicted is a real Venice personality.

166. *Venice in Snow,* 1970. The scene depicted is located about a half mile north of the painting and is identical to the view of that location from the Venice boardwalk. However, there is one slight alteration of reality—the snow on the ground. It has never snowed in Venice. Venice in Snow became a victim of construction only two years after it was created—a dingbat apartment house was built six inches away on the adjoining lot, totally obscuring the mural.

167. The Isle of California, located on Butler Avenue in West Los Angeles, was commissioned by Gordie Hormel, a businessman who paid $20,000 to have the side wall of his recording studio

immortalized. The image of the severed freeway was conceived by the Los Angeles Fine Arts Squad prior to the major 1971 earthquake. Since then, the irony of the painting has increased considerably.

168. The *Brooks Street Painting,* 1969, Venice.

169. Reality across the vacant lot, 1969, Venice.

170 - 172. *The Beverly Hills Siddhartha,* 9,000 square feet of curving wall space, begun in 1969 and finished in 1970 at a cost of $15,000 and 200 gallons of paint. This, the second painting by the Los Angeles Fine Arts Squad, was a work of technical and conceptual brilliance which succeeded in visually obliterating the Climax Club's bizarre structure as well as communicating a parable of a modern-day Siddhartha.

173. Two-story portrait of actor Steve McQueen by Kent Twitchell on Union Street near Venice Boulevard.

174. Kent Twitchell received college art class credit for his impressive painting of character actor Strother Martin. Located in Hollywood on the corner of Fountain Avenue and Kingsley Drive, the muultiple portrait suggests an impressionistic application of the photographic technique. The mural is approximately twelve feet high.

175. The Great Pig Mural on the Farmer John brand, Clougherty Meat Packing Company's facilities in East Los Angeles. The mural sprawls over the entire length of the multiple block meat-packing plant and is a totally impressionistic view of "Hog Heaven" as seen through the eyes of the late Les Grimes. An Austrian immigrant and former movie sign painter, Grimes worked on the mural for eleven years until 1968, when he fell to his death from a scaffold while completing an area of sky in that "Great Farmland Vista." Following Grimes' death, Barney Clougherty hired Arno Jordon, also an Austrian immigrant, to finish the mural. "In all innocence, the great Pig Mural has become a metaphor of a life of luxury and affluence led in ignorance of the price it exacts," said Wilson in the *Los Angeles Times.* The tree to the right side of the photograph is a real twelve-foot tree provided by the City of Los Angeles.

176. Mural "photographic collage" entitled *Venice High Yearbook, Class of '53* by Arthur Mortimer. The painting is inside the Venice Pavilion at the end of Windward Avenue in Venice and is part of a community project organized by Judy Grupp of the city park staff.

177. The Great Pig Mural, revealing the reality behind the facade.

178. Detail of the symbol of the former Aquarius Theater, now the Moulin Rouge, on the Sunset Strip. The mural covered the entire building and was painted by a group of Dutch and English artists called "The Fool." The site of the Los Angeles performances of the rock musical "Hair," the Aquarius rapidly became a Hollywood landmark. The painting depicted, in rainbow-psychedelic style, the coming of the Age of Aquarius. Unfortunately, the theater walls were not washed and primed properly before paint was applied, and, after a year and a half, the painting began to peel and was finally painted out in 1971.

179. *Two Girls,* 1970, Wayne Holwick's latest, largest, and most technically competent work, was painted out in 1974. The mural was approximately ten feet high.

180. Kent Twitchell's most recent mural, painted for the Inner City Mural Program. He describes the painting as "a monument to old age." He chose character actress Lillian Bronson as the model for the old woman. (She was the original judge on the Perry Mason series and has appeared frequently in both films and television.) Twitchell feels that, by using character actors, his murals become more accessible to people. "Their face is an open door into the subconscious. People are familiar with them but don't know who they are," he explains. The mural is located on the northeast wall of a building at Temple Street and Edgeware Road and is easily seen by motorists driving west on the Hollywood Freeway.

181. *Groupie,* 1968, by Wayne Holwick. This was the first significant wall painting in the Venice "hip" community. *Groupie* remained unmarred by graffiti until the artist himself whitewashed it in 1975 to prevent people from selling paintings of the image.

182. Union 76 ball and Hollywood sign. Hollywood, 1976. Photograph by Alex Hajdu.

183. Harbor Freeway in downtown Los Angeles rush hour. Photograph by Roger Webster.

184. Refinery and car dealership next to the San Diego Freeway. Photograph by Terrance Ford.

185. Police helicopter over Hollywood. Photograph by Jed Wilcox, 1973.

186. Hollywood Freeway, rush hour. Photograph by John Bright.

187. Photograph by Susan Sullivan, 1975.

188. San Diego Freeway near Torrance. Photograph by Terrance Ford.

1,500 copies of this catalog designed by John Coy, typeset by Fotoset Inc.,
have been printed by Alan Printing & Litho, Los Angeles, in January 1977
for Museum Associates of the Los Angeles County Museum of Art.

124